Introduction to Humanistic Psychology

Charlotte Bühler
and
Melanie Allen

BROOKS/COLE PUBLISHING COMPANY
Monterey, California
A Division of Wadsworth Publishing Company, Inc.
Belmont, California

M

ISBN: 0-8185-0032-8

L.C. Catalog Card No: 72-77603

Printed in the United States of America

4 5 6 7 8 9 10—76

This book was edited by Mary Vandervoort, with production supervised by Micky Stay. It was designed by Linda Marcetti. The book was typeset by Datagraphics, Inc., Phoenix, Arizona, and printed and bound by Malloy Lithography, Ann Arbor, Michigan.

This book was written
with the deep hope and conviction
that humanistic psychology
can help
the torn culture
of our time
as we have seen it help
many
of our own students and patients.

Preface

In 1962 Abraham Maslow called for the founding of an organization to represent what he saw as a "third force" in psychology—that is, a stream of psychological thought and an image of man that differed from those of both psychoanalysis and behaviorism. This new school, called humanistic psychology, attracted members from many backgrounds and divergent disciplines. Yet all agreed that a new thrust was needed to combat and challenge the growing social and cultural crisis and the feelings of dehumanization and deindividualization of the twentieth century.

In the decade since its inception, humanistic psychology has spread rapidly over the United States, its birthplace, and has begun to grow in other countries. However, the new school has received major criticism, even from within its own ranks. Humanistic psychology has been accused of being vague and unscientific in structure and goals.

This book attempts to present a systematic formulation of the goals, methodology, and theoretical bases of the new approach to man. We begin by tracing the origins of humanistic psychology back to its philosophical "mother," humanism, and by discussing the relationship of humanistic psychology to the contemporary philosophical orientation of existentialism. From this historical picture, we turn to the current theoretical structure of the new school in an attempt to justify its status as a science, both statistically and methodologically. Finally, we discuss the relevance of this new position and its goals in terms of the current cultural crisis.

We wish to express our appreciation to Ernest Keen of Bucknell University for his helpful reviews of the manuscript. We would also like to thank Margaret Levers, R. Craig Bühler, and McLaughlin Smith, for permitting us to quote their poems and dialogue, and Jette Toft and Clarice Garfin, for their invaluable help in preparation of the manuscript.

Charlotte Bühler
Melanie Allen

Contents

viii

Introduction
Why the widespread interest
in humanistic psychology?

The name *humanistic psychology* was chosen by a group of psychologists who in 1962 joined under the leadership of Abraham Maslow to found a new association. The main purpose of this organization and of a journal bearing the same name, edited by Anthony Sutich since 1961, was to explore the behavioral characteristics and emotional dynamics of *full and healthy human living.* Bühler and Bugental formulated a statement of those characteristics common to exponents of this orientation. The Association of Humanistic Psychology, while admitting to a lack of complete unanimity in this regard, publishes these four elements:

1. A centering of attention on the experiencing *person,* and thus a focus on experience as the primary phenomenon in the study of man. Both theoretical explanations and overt behavior are considered secondary to experience itself and to its meaning to the person.
2. An emphasis on such distinctively human qualities as choice, creativity, valuation, and self-realization, as opposed to thinking about human beings in mechanistic and reductionistic terms.
3. An allegiance to meaningfulness in the selection of problems for study and of research procedures, and an opposition to a

primary emphasis on objectivity at the expense of significance.
4. An ultimate concern with and valuing of the dignity and
worth of man and an interest in the development of the
potential inherent in every person. Central in this view is the
person as he discovers his own being and relates to other
persons and to social groups.

The Brochure of the AHP

The representatives of this "Third Force," as Maslow
called it (in comparison with behavioristic and psychoanalytic
psychology), shared certain convictions about healthy human life
which differed from those of the two other psychological schools.
They also developed new approaches to the study of the person
and new methods of psychotherapy, based on their different understanding of people. Recently their viewpoint has also influenced the practical worlds of business, industry, education, and
administration. In its interpretation of human life, humanistic
psychology encompasses a philosophy—a view of what life is
about and what life can be, if lived constructively.

Many persons who may have only superficial acquaint-
ance with the ideas and methods of humanistic psychology feel
vaguely that this is a view of human existence with which they
can identify, which will help them to find themselves and to
clarify their own thinking. Young people—and older people who
still dare to search and discover—are attracted to humanistic psychology for its emphasis on inner freedom, self-expression, and
expansion. They gain from its belief in the personal worth of the
individual and in creativity as a basic force, as well as from its
emphasis on development toward self-realization—that state of
being which calls for a self-transcendence in which the individual
encompasses his fellow-men.

The problems of our time are increasing, and solutions to
life often seem beyond our reach. Confrontation with the issues
of today has become a way of life for many people; yet others are
able simply to accept their lives, not asking these universal questions so relevant to our contemporary dilemma concerning the
human condition.

Recently a lady scoffed at an article on campus unrest:
"All this is just adolescent rebellion." One sensed her hostility
toward the upheaval in our society. Her reaction to a group acting-

out of this turmoil is not uncommon. She did not understand that underlying the more extreme, sensational actions she reads about, many people are searching within, hoping to discover a new basis for their beliefs and values and, in many instances, a reason for life itself. One must return to the period of the Reformation and the Renaissance for a parallel to this present crisis in Western civilization.

This crisis is not sudden and abrupt. It has been developing for a long time. It has been brewing in Europe since the beginning of this century. Many European youth felt then, as American students do now, that we live with great hypocrisy, under the aegis of a religious and moral code adhered to only superficially. Few people, they feel, reflect seriously upon the meaning of human life and how one can live life fully. More and more, the conviction has grown that religious and moral traditions have been passed along with scant reexamination of basic principles. Criticism of their ineffectiveness in the arena of life has become consistent in contemporary dialogue. Refusal to give allegiance to authority, regardless of competence and the validity of the views and actions of that authority, is no longer taboo. European youth, reading Hesse almost a half-century ago, recognized the industrial dehumanization of life. Now American youth has taken up that cry which previously was a silent whisper in our nation—a cry which speaks of the need to rejuvenate those qualities in existence which are life-giving and life-sustaining.

American youth asks for and fights for genuine, honest, human, and humane ways of living. Humanistic psychology supports this plea in its philosophical, psychological, and ethical tenets. It hopes to play a major role in helping to bring about those metamorphoses necessary to the survival of man. It also hopes that its inherent belief in the ability of individual man to create meaning out of absurdity will serve as a positive force in contemporary life.

1
Science and culture

One cannot understand any thesis concerning life without considering the context within which it evolved. Science did not exist before man; science was created by man. Just so, its developments and metamorphoses reflect the changes of men, the manner in which they gradually come to perceive their world differently and to change their life-styles.

The social and cultural contexts create in man the need to focus on certain factors of life. He studies the environment—and himself *in* the environment—to seize upon the essentials of his own existence. K. B. Madsen's lucid statement (1970) about the metatheoretical position of the scientist and its influence on his choice of focus and hypothesis expresses our own feelings.

Madsen's work is valuable to us because it confronts the scientist (and the human being) with the fact that he does not work in hermetic isolation. Today a humanistically oriented scientist *must*, it would seem, spend time and energy on pursuits which acknowledge the necessity for reasonable action in this current culture crisis. We are reminded of the symbolic and unforgettable picture sketched by Bronowski (1965) in describing the "universal moment" wherein, as scientist, he discovered "on a fine November day" the skeletal ghost of Nagasaki. Bronowski remembers with irony: "We looked up and saw the power of which we had been proud loom over us like the ruins of Nagasaki," and from a ship in the nearby harbor someone could be heard singing *Is You Is Or Is You Ain't My Baby?*

In this chapter we present a brief summary of the work of Madsen as it represents our own view of the philosophy of science and cultural history. We then turn to a consideration of the current American cultural complex.

A. *Philosophy of science and cultural history*

The attempt of humanistic psychology to prove itself as a valid scientific approach may also be seen from a philosophical point of view. Maslow (1966) and Giorgi (1970) are also of this opinion. Madsen (1970)* states that every scientific methodology proceeds from the concept of man and science in a certain time and culture. In his comparative study of psychological theories, he comes to the conclusion that humanistic psychology "represents a new and broader philosophy of science, and that humanistic psychology shares in a 'revolution' in the philosophy of science with other philosophical trends of European origin" (p. 1). According to him, "this new emerging philosophy of science is the product of a long development of the psychologist's conception of his own science" (p. 1).

Every scientific theory, Madsen feels, has its philosophical counterpart in "metatheory." In discussions with Allport and Maslow, he became convinced that every psychologist has a presupposed concept of man, which may not be verbalized but which influences research and theory construction. This concept proceeds from the philosophy of a specific time, as it develops in a specific cultural period and climate.

Thus in *empiricism,* observation is considered the main source of knowledge, and its ideal emerged as experimental science. Psychology accepted this ideal and model. For that reason Wundt's classic experimental psychology was purely descriptive. Phenomena of the conscious mind were observed, and "laws" about their relationships were formulated. Mere explanatory hy-

*A presentation at the First International Conference on Humanistic Psychology, Amsterdam, 1970; published in the *Journal of Humanistic Psychology,* 1971, **11** (1).

potheses were considered unscientific. This method was applied to European structural psychology and later to American behaviorism.

Madsen considers Freud the first psychologist to construct a psychological model, in his attempt to explain dreams.

With the neobehaviorists Tolman (1932) and Hull (1943) and with the field-theorist Lewin (1936), this philosophy of science gained acceptance (Koch, 1959) from 1930 to 1960. In this period statements of facts and laws were included with hypothetical explanations using hypothetical constructions or models. We find this same model-building in Karl Bühler's *Sprachtheorie* (Speech Theory) (1965) and in his *Krise der Psychologie* (Crisis of Psychology) (1927) as well as in Charlotte Bühler's developmental theory in *Kindheit und Jugend* (Childhood and Adolescence) (1928) and *Der menschliche Lebenslauf als psychologisches Problem* (The Course of Human Life as a Psychological Problem) (1933). Several other developmental theories were also model-building, notably those of Piaget, Werner, and Erikson.

But in the period in which humanistic psychology has developed, "the main thesis in the theory of science is that *scientific theories are part of the whole cultural context*" (Madsen, 1970, p. 4). This is a "metatheory," which lies behind every scientific theory.

Madsen finds that a "philosophy of man" is the basis for a complete psychological theory and, specifically, for humanistic psychology. It influences research and theory construction, even if it is unverbalized. Yet Madsen suggests that the philosophy *should* be verbalized to bring into the open the actual presuppositions from which a scientific procedure starts. Madsen also refers to Kuhn (1962), who demonstrated that scientific theory and research have a prescientific frame of reference. Kuhn shows that the "normal" scientific act is that of following certain predetermined steps geared toward the discovery and elaboration of models or *paradigms*. Kuhn believes that "sharing in the study of paradigms" prepares one for membership in the scientific community. The choice of models, however, and the method of study were passed on as the scientific tradition—and science itself—became a model, against which few have dared to propose nonnormative procedures and materials for study.

Madsen quotes recent European thinkers who stress the relationship of science to the whole philosophy of man and society at a certain time and to the value system inherent in this philosophy. He mentions the Frankfurt school as well as some Swedish thinkers, especially Radnitzky (1968). We might note that this latter author has accomplished the mammoth task of collecting the works of all major thinkers in the philosophy of science and proposing innovative suggestions for integrating much of their thought. Madsen also refers to Joseph Royce's investigations, which stress the psychological factors that determine all theorizing.

Madsen himself terms his conviction "integrative rationalism," a "philosophy of science, the essence of which is that *scientific hypotheses and theories are products of thinking but inspired by the intuition formulated in philosophy and other cultural factors, and tested by empirical methods*" (p. 9).

B. The current American cultural complex

We have established our belief that one cannot understand psychological theory without considering the cultural context within which it develops. Although we shall devote a later chapter to a more detailed consideration of contemporary culture, we think it essential to present a look at the cultural situation within which many scientific innovations are so rapidly developing.

The evolution in the American attitude itself has been apparent to those who once characterized the American people as notably optimistic. What events and developments contributed to increasing pessimism in Americans? What challenged their great hope?

Perhaps the first and most encompassing issue is war, with its resultant despair over humanity's continuing drive toward aggression and self-destruction. Our youth's growing awareness of and involvement in the basic experience of mankind, linked with the expanding availability of information to the masses, have led to a major change in our attitudes toward war.

One of the profound experiences in this century has been the impact of the succession of wars in which youth everywhere were required to participate and which continue to shock the world with the destruction and disaster they have produced. The term *world war* was in no way a misnomer, for the world has indeed been irretrievably changed by the wars and grim weapons of this century. This change is brought home to us powerfully in *Oh, What a Lovely War!*, a movie adapted from the play of the same title by the British playwright Joan Greenwood. It sarcastically describes the euphoria and frivolity with which "responsible" leaders and blind followers fell into World War I, as though it were a summer picnic at the seashore. In contrast to this attitude, once embraced in the name of patriotism and duty, we now find total worldwide rejection of war for war's sake or even for country's sake. Simultaneously, we see overt expressions of anger and revolt at being forced into this sort of destructive involvement with no respect for an individual's philosophy.

A number of factors contributed to this development. World War II, coming so soon after World War I, was perhaps the turning point in altering the American philosophy of determined optimism. For all those who had expected the twentieth century to end war, World War II represented civilization's greatest disillusionment. The whole world was tormented by the cause of the war and its far-reaching ramifications, and Americans were in no way immune to the deep marks it left. Out of this "social anxiety" Karen Horney and Erich Fromm emerged to ask us "Can we trust society?" And certainly the terroristic cruelties in Russia after Stalin's takeover, those in Hitler's Germany, and those to come in Vietnam with the sacrifice of thousands of people and such massacres as My Lai, left questions almost too horrible to be faced— basic questions about the nature of man and his impulses.

Doubts concerning the moral progress of humanity, dread of the bomb, and fear of mankind's possible self-destruction developed. In *On the Beach* Nevil Shute described this constant terror realistically and dramatically, and, in Stanley Kramer's film adaptation the threat to individual existence is starkly revealed when the young wife prepares to take her own life and that of her baby, rather than face the slow death of radiation. She whispers to her husband "I loved you *so* much." "I loved you so much," in the past tense, as though to say: "I had so much. We all had so much. And it has all been taken away and will never happen again. . . . Life —human life—will never happen again."

We were suddenly confronted with the true status of our government and with the fact that we were not forever safe in our stronghold but were exposed to long-camouflaged irritations and injustices in our culture. The unwillingness of many blacks and whites to accept the traditional double standard of rich-poor forced many seriously to question their beliefs about democracy. On the issue of poverty, attacks were waged against political leadership as well as against many of the rich—against all who had permitted so much poverty to persist in this most affluent of world societies. It was felt that to preach Christian charity and at the same time to do so little for people living in starvation and miserable conditions were flagrantly hypocritical. Industrialism's exploitation of human beings was held responsible. Masses of young people displayed their rebellion by withdrawing from work altogether. At first the passive resistance of youth was an attempt to demonstrate scorn of the Establishment. The ethic of Christian love was expressed in communal life among peers. Some took refuge in Eastern philosophies. But the difficulty of maintaining such material-*less* subcultures in the midst of our Great Society (in terms of number and wealth) makes these efforts appear to be a rather helpless, doomed cry of defiance in a large and impersonal culture.

By putting the accent on the younger generation in this discussion of issues, we do not mean to indicate that students and young people are the exclusive fighters in these areas. Because of repeated stress on these issues, more thoughtful coverage by the media, and the developing logic, strong arguments, and effectiveness of what was becoming an active rather than a passive movement, many older people joined in the attack. But there is no doubt that the initial impetus and continued enthusiasm were tremendously enhanced by the vigorous, uncompromising activities of more and more young people.

Closely related to the poverty issue is that of racial discrimination, which, with the Supreme Court's proclamation in the fifties, came to the foreground of the American scene. Still unresolved despite endless debates and violent outbursts, it rocks the nation. The Watts Riot of 1965, though not the first race riot, was *recognized* as a blemish on our nation's history. Rioting, the fear of violence, and the presence of guardsmen and police are now part of our country's life-style.

Tremendous as these problems are, however, and far-reaching as their impact is on our nation's cohesion and dignity, they may be surpassed by the tremendous problems of sex and love in our present culture. Love is a necessary component in a complete life and a defense against the painful feelings of isolation, loneliness, and absurdity of twentieth-century living. It is ironic that when we need it so much, it seems as impossible for some to make "love" as to end war. And, because many have never achieved this emotion, it is difficult for them to separate love from sex; they hope that if they can educate themselves to natural and comfortable sexual relationships, love also will come to them. Nothing is more chronic in this culture than the continued conflict engendered by this problem, especially as it affects marital relationships.

The movie *Bob & Carol & Ted & Alice* (1969) is a successful attempt to illustrate the rather feverish emancipation process that spread over the United States in the decade of the sixties. Students and young marrieds of that era "discovered" a solution to the lack of satisfaction, emptiness, and shallowness of life characteristic of the postwar fifties. They were trying to rebuild an existence that had been fundamentally grounded in "safe prosperity" and its material by-products—an existence sapped of a strong and deep value system. The development of the *Esalen movement,* with its emphasis on free expression and touch, the dropping of defenses, and a striving for "awareness," represented to many the possibility of enhancing a bland existence and, indeed, a promise of richer love potential.

The distinctive factor in this move, however, is the gradual realization that the formal entry into a "sensitive period of life" for these young (and often subtly desperate) people has become just another frantic attempt; the extremism with which they pursue their deliberate goal of openness is as doomed and as unrewarding to their lives as was their previous obsession with large wardrobes and status symbols. In other words, they pursue freedom and awareness with a vengeance, and the pursuit of freedom with a vengeance obviously lacks the very spontaneity and depth inherent and implicit in the concept of "freedom."

Near the end of *Bob & Carol & Ted & Alice,* when the two couples have seemingly attained the pinnacle of their "experiment with life" and are about to give way to their "feelings" in a four-way bed party, there is a sudden, shattering silence. They look sadly, shamefacedly, at one another and at us, as if to say "My God, what have we done? This time, like all the other times, we have gone too far. Why? Where are we *now*?" Presented with a light touch, the film is a tragic, gray black portrait in Technicolor of a well-intentioned effort gone disastrously astray. Allen (1970a) has described, in an article for the lay reader, the sadness inherent in the faddist exploitation of a movement which, although originally meant to heal, may actually pour more salt on the wounds.

This issue of increasing the quantity of feelings, despite an inability by many to deal with the qualitative content of emotions, is also related to the current demand for expanded awareness and stronger sensory experiences than exist in everyday life. In taking drugs, for instance, now an integral part of the youth culture, there is a twofold motivation: (1) to extend one's self through expanding one's experience and (2) to rebel, as Sid Jourard put it, against the pattern of the Establishment.

Over and above all these very human problems is one to which we have contributed by our inventiveness and ingenuity and which may, some feel, now be out of control. This is the problem of the earth itself and of ecology—of whether we as a species will be able to live on a poisoned planet. Mary, who is 26, says "I really don't ever expect to live past 40. By then the world will be finished." Here we confront a danger perhaps even more threatening than war, which we like to think could be stopped. But how shall we stop this present threat? Szent-Györgyi (1970) sadly sums up this confrontation of our youth with the problems of today:

> What (our youth) learn of the world as they grow up, is markedly different from what children of the pre-War world learned. . . . For what do they see? Going to their classrooms they have to pass their school air raid shelters, which experience reminds them that one day their whole world may be wiped out. They are driven to the conclusion that there is no value in endeavor and that the only wise thing to do is to enjoy the moment, enjoy their growing bodies, enjoy what life can offer so long as it lasts.

In questioning society's values, youth in America began to extend their attacks to the educational system, unveiling its inadequacies and, in some cases, injustices. The college campus, formerly safe from the struggles of the political arena, became the primary forum from which youth confronted the older generation.

(The attempt to build new and innovative educational systems will be elaborated upon in a later chapter of this book.)

Other groups in our nation gained courage from the growth of the civil rights movement and the youth revolution and began to plead for justice in its own right. Women renewed the struggle for equal rights with men, and the Women's Liberation Movement spread to Europe and to Russia. Minority groups fought in the courts and picketed on the streets to end oppression and gain recognition that would lead to revision of old laws and provision for a life free from stigma. Former prisoners, religious groups, and homosexuals joined the struggle.

Szent-Györgyi believes that if youth feels any sense of power at all in this diminishing era, it must muster that power to fight "for a better world right now." Charles Hampden-Turner's illuminating document *Radical Man* (1970) elaborates upon this thesis. Hampden-Turner compares the solid core of the contemporary radical, who is firm in his ideals and his dedication and therefore clear as to his identity and his purpose, with Maslow's *self-actualized* individual (1961).

At such a time, when old methods for dealing with life problems seem ineffective, when old values are questioned, when all people seek new ways of coping with human life as a whole, we understand humanistic psychology's great appeal. No psychology as such can provide a philosophy for all men; but humanistic psychology is perhaps in a better position to help, since it focuses on the discovery of principles that have proved constructive in achieving and maintaining meaningful lives and since it allows room for *each* individual to grasp those principles and those potentialities most useful to *him* in the rebuilding of his own life.

This seems to be what most of us have sought: if not a "whole new philosophy," at least some general principles which will help us, given our own particular requirements for satisfaction and contentment, to experience personal meaning in our lives, despite the fact that the ultimate meaning of life itself may elude us.

2
The historical roots of humanistic psychology

Although humanistic psychology is a science, it is clearly different from other psychological systems in that it emphasizes certain *philosophical* theories about man. This is one of the most significant and distinctive characteristics of this contemporary system of psychology.

Various orientations in psychology, notably Wundtian "structural psychology," Freud's psychoanalytic school, and Watsonian behaviorism, continue to take pride in their independence of philosophy. In contrast, humanistic psychology criticizes theories of human life that stress those mechanical aspects of human functioning which take the physical sciences as models. Although repeated attempts have been made, particularly by German psychologists, to emphasize the factors of meaning and value in human life (as opposed to viewing the mind as a mechanism), they previously had not led to fully developed systems of psychology or were not able to prove the scientific validity of their methods and concepts, although certain theoreticians like Dilthey and Spranger in Germany made concentrated efforts on treatment of this problem.

In humanistic psychology, many psychologists from different backgrounds came together to demonstrate human living and behavior as a comprehensive system in which values, goals, and meaning play essential roles. They hoped to establish that the significance of these factors could be demonstrated with scientifically valid methods and concepts. This approach brought psychology back to a close relationship with philosophy—that is, it emphasized systematic speculations concerning the universe and human existence within the universe.

Two philosophical systems to which humanistic psychology is closely related are *existentialism* and *humanism*. A brief historical presentation of these systems may serve as an introduction to our study of humanistic psychology as a science that leads to practical conclusions for living. This short survey will help us to understand how existentialistic and humanistic psychology emerged from what in the United States until the 1950s was largely a behavioristically or psychoanalytically oriented science.

A. Premodern humanism

The humanism with which we are familiar today—a broad, philosophical approach to man and existence—can be traced to Socrates' beliefs regarding education and the individual. Love of "liberty" and the "open forum" as an arena for freedom of expression typified the ideals of Socrates and his student Plato and became a principle of the Greek and Roman republics.

Humanism as a specific intellectual movement originated in protest against the rigid Scholasticism of the Middle Ages. The movement began with the School of Chartres, wherein there was greater admiration for the Socratic method of education than for the Aristotelian, which emphasized a more scholastic approach. The Scholastics of the Middle Ages were religionists: priests and monks. They followed prescribed methods of learning and studied according to prescribed traditions. The Scholastics were in fact associated with the Church, and the humanistic movement, as it became a mainstream in the Renaissance, was often considered an anti-Church movement. In truth, however, as Bertrand Russell points out, the attitudes of the anti-Scholastic members of the humanistic movement varied; some actually made peace with the Church, if only at the approach of death. Yet the movement was a distinct break with the medieval scholastic system of thinking that Church philosophers had developed.

An interesting early effect of the movement was the retention of religion's superstitious aspects (another return to antiquity perhaps). Astrology was especially favored by these freethinkers. Bertrand Russell (1945) states that "the first effect of emancipation from the Church was not to make men think rationally, but to open their minds to every sort of antique nonsense." Because of this interest, many of the humanists were considered to lead "black lives," and in fact the rise of humanism led to a simultaneous rise of paganism. This may remind us of current, off-shoot "humanistic" movements, whose members use the excuse that they are gaining self-knowledge to justify eccentric, unconventional behavior. Russell stated that "the old moral rules ceased to be respected," and in truth even in the humanistic Popes of Italy there was a marked period of experimentation with life. Perhaps for this reason the outstanding achievements of the period were not in philosophy, (although the movement opened the door to independent critical thinking), but in the arts. Why was this so? Why was there a spurt of artistic expression? Perhaps it issued out of this new respect for independent thought, which led to the concept that there could be different opinions and interpretations of the same subject.

Although Petrarch was considered the "father of humanism," scholars of this period consider him only the "first figure." For example, Cassirer, Kristeller, and Randall (1948) emphasize that the value set which we now call "humanistic" was incidental to the original movement, whose emphasis was on classical studies. The name *humanist* was borrowed from the focus of studies, *Studia Humanitas,* or the humanities. To the humanists the classics represented the highest level of human achievement, and knowledge of the classics would lead to the development of highly desirable human beings. "The humanists tried and managed to express the concrete circumstances of their own life and personal thoughts and feelings in a language largely borrowed from classical models" (Cassirer et al., 1948). Petrarch maintained that logical and natural philosophies were not important to man and his eventual destiny; he emphasized man's dignity and glorification. This early trend of the humanistic movement was to be renewed in the twentieth century.

Nicholas V (1447–1455) was the first humanist Pope, and he encouraged humanism over pious orthodoxy and the traditional attitudes toward morals and religion. For instance, he allowed criticism of the sacrosanct Vulgate, the accepted translation of the Bible.

Perhaps this early humanism's most direct relation to present humanistic thinking in the sciences, and especially psychology, is found in the works of Erasmus of Rotterdam, the archetypal writer and representative of humanistic thought in the Renaissance. His book *On Free Will* is considered by many scholars to be the great book of that period and the impetus behind the Reformation movement. Winter (1961), discussing the free thought movement, writes: "Erasmus laid the egg which Luther hatched." In Erasmus' book we find that same struggle for the establishment and definition of "inner freedom" which many psychologists today hold to be central and integral. But whereas the earlier school sought this inner freedom between the covers of old books, today we try to secure it for ourselves experientially, in the act of living.

Intent upon the concept of freedom, Erasmus disliked the idea of attachment to any philosophy at all. He was perhaps an extreme example of his movement, just as today we have analogous examples. The original movement, however, was primarily intellectual.

Erasmus was highly religious, but he believed in man's essential freedom and the creative power of the individual. In this way he differed from Martin Luther, who stated that man was unable to choose not to commit sin without the intervention of God's grace. However, although Erasmus believed in God, he did not believe in the idea of "religion as a system" and in this respect was against the Church. Originally a monk, he felt stultified by the atmosphere of the monastic scholar and became anti-Aristotelian and antididactic. Christianity for Erasmus was not the "dogmatic religion" it remained to Luther but rather a concept of "morality, a simplicity of life and of doctrine" (Winter, 1961).

In discussing free will, Erasmus wrote: "By freedom of the will we understand in this connection the power of the human will whereby man can apply to or turn away from that which leads unto eternal salvation." Here Erasmus makes a simple statement for the basic existential freedom of man. Man has, in his terms, the choice of whether or not he wishes to be saved. God may save man, but man decides if he wants to put his life in God's hands. To Erasmus free will was therefore a vital part of the life of man. This idea had great influence on many of the philosophers to follow, such as Leibnitz and Kant.

B. Existentialism

Another contemporary approach to mankind is that of the existentialists, who represent several widespread revolts against traditional philosophy. Many of the precepts of existentialism can be found in the beliefs of humanistically oriented scientists, and this movement has had great impact on the twentieth century.

In the introduction to his anthology on existentialism, Kaufmann (1956) stresses that it is "not a school of thought nor reducible to any set of tenets. . . . It is (rather) a refusal to belong to any school of thought, the repudiation of the adequacy of any body of beliefs whatever, and *especially of systems*, and a marked dissatisfaction with traditional philosophy as superficial, academic, and *remote from life*" (italics ours).

The emphasis on individuality issued directly from the influence of the earlier Romantic movement, but the existential movement is free from the rather adolescent, self-pitying, antisocial attitude of the classic romanticists. Kaufmann, in fact, views the romantic movement as escapist. Perhaps it is analogous to the present-day hippie culture in this regard. But, whereas the romanticists gained their escape through "deliverance from the cross of Here and Now" (Kaufmann, 1956), young people today seek deliverance from confrontation with the future. Both, in a sense, refuse to accept the full scope and spectrum of actual existence.

Kierkegaard, whose major writings appeared in the 1840s, is usually considered the founder of existentialism as we know it today. Horner and Bühler (1969), surveying his contributions, wrote:

> Kierkegaard saw the coming alienation of man from himself . . . and pointed out that "the meaning for the person of the objective fact . . . depends on how he relates to it; there is now existential truth which can omit the relationship. . . . When we

are dealing with human beings, no truth has reality by itself; it is always dependent upon the reality of the immediate relationship." This is not to say that the existential view is that of the philosophical idealist, for facts are acknowledged as being real. A tree is a tree—although its meaning to the man who views it ("the truth") depends upon his relationship to it. Does it give him fruit or shade, or is it an obstacle in his path?

Kierkegaard also emphasized the necessity for *commitment,* believing that "one could not be an objective disinterested observer, but that one could only see a particular truth if he had some commitment to it" (May, 1958). One quickly sees the similarity of this idea to phenomenology. But it is not essentially a phenomenological position, for Kierkegaard does not say "The chair is there and *I* see it this way, though you see it that way." He is subjective in orientation, but not an extreme subjective idealist like Berkeley.

Kaufmann states that, although Kierkegaard felt "the world had no part in helping man with the 'human condition,'" he would not classify Kierkegaard as a romantic because he ". . . rejects the dim twilight of sentiment as well as any lovely synthesis of intellect and feeling, to insist on the absurdity of the beliefs which he accepts." Kierkegaard was against "any calculation without the individual" and so rejected the Greek heritage largely because of its insistence on logic and mathematical reasoning.

The human condition, said Kierkegaard, is a state of need which requires choice and decision. One's ethics operate not simply as a manner of evaluating a situation, but rather as an active factor in the decision-making process. He says "I experience dread in the dizziness of my freedom, and my choice is made in fear and trembling." (See Lowrie, 1938.)

It seems that this very emphasis on ethics and on the decision-making process is what caused Heidegger to dismiss Kierkegaard as merely a religious writer. Heidegger was strongly influenced by Nietzsche but, although cognizant of and emphatic as to the limitations of science, clearly attempted to put his own ideas into a more systematic context than the fluid, literary discourse of Nietzsche. Heidegger had an ability to create terminology, and this in itself made him a kind of systemologist. Heidegger is given credit, with Jaspers, for the founding of formal existential philosophy. His main concern was with fundamental ontology, which he interpreted as the study of being and the essence of being itself. His analysis of man's existence included the basic inquiry "Why is there any Being at all and not rather nothing?" (1929).

Kaufmann (1956) points out that the interesting trend in Heidegger's study is his gradual change of focus. Although originally he tried to comprehend being directly, later he attempted to study this condition through scholarly consideration of texts. Heidegger's followers believed his major contribution to be a demonstration of "the temporality of man's existence, that he strikes new paths by raising the question of Being itself." He disagrees with Descartes' dualistic conception of the human organism.

It is interesting that neither Heidegger nor Jaspers cared to be called an "existentialist," as Sartre was. Heidegger (1947) wrote an interesting response to Sartre's lecture of 1946, "Existentialism Is a Humanism," saying that Sartre's paradigm, "existence before essence," was still a "metaphysical sentence" and did not cohere with his own philosophy, which focused on "Being" itself. By this, Heidegger emphasizes his own loyalty to the search for that essence of being which is beyond the being of any one man, and so he departs from Sartre's philosophy. Heidegger's desire to touch that being "of which we are all a part" is perhaps more Eastern in orientation than Western.

Jaspers (1938) also emphasized the limitations of science and named his approach to being *Existenzphilosophie.* He stated his argument against systems of philosophy which he believed were restrictive: "Philosophy can never wish to be less than primordial, eternal philosophy itself." He fought dualism and harshly attacked Christianity. His criticism of the sciences is aimed directly at psychology. He says: "Who before me among philosophers has been a psychologist?" Kaufmann feels that Jaspers' antidoctrinaire attitude led him from philosophy to philosophizing, and Jaspers probably would have agreed, for he wrote: "In a sense, I say nothing."

Sartre, who popularized existentialism, brought thinking back to Kierkegaard by returning to the human condition and the absurdity of human life, as well as to the tragic fact that we are required to form commitments and make decisions without proper knowledge of their consequences for us and for others. In contrast to earlier thinkers, Sartre considers his writings psychological. He discusses despair, decision, dread, and self-deception as based on experience (*L 'Être et le néant,* 1943). His own fictional writings are applications of and/or contributions to his theory.

Sartre emphasizes *choice* as the main aspect of human life, but he insists that man's tragic situation does not rule out "integrity of choice" in opposition to choices of "social utility" (that which is socially functional). Like Shakespeare, Sartre says: "There are situations in which, whatever choice we make, we cannot escape guilt." This may remind psychotherapists of situations arising in the lives of patients who are experiencing conflict among various choices: they convince themselves that each one carries its own particular sacrifice, its own residual of guilt.

Attempting to find central agreement among all these thinkers, Kaufmann states: "All of them contrast inauthentic life and authentic life . . . (all believed that) to be serious, *a philosophy has to be lived.*" This point shows a significant agreement between existential thinkers and the humanistic psychologists.

A further philosophical link is found in the works of Albert Camus, the noted French Nobel Prize winner whose own species of existentialism was to depart markedly from that of Sartre in the years preceding his early death. In his fiction Camus paints what some feel is a pessimistic picture of life. Meursault, *L 'Etranger* (The Stranger) (1942), represents man alienated from life and even from his own feelings, awakened only at the approach of his execution. Meursault's entire existence is one of hazy apathy, of life without hope. In *La Peste* (The Plague) (1947), the citizens await death at any moment, which again seems to emphasize the absurdity of existence. To travel full circle with Camus, however, one must read his essays—his journey into his own soul —particularly those revolving around his native Algiers.

It is noteworthy that Camus chose to be called "humanist" rather than "existentialist" in later years. One understands this distinction by reading his essays. We might say that he replaces the meaning in life, which had earlier been stripped away by Sartre. Why do we feel this to be so? Because our experience of Camus in the essays is of a human being, a writer, a philosopher so elevating the moment of experience, both specifically and generally, that man, and creative man in particular, is able to gain salvation by creating salvation, moment by moment. Camus believes this is part of the life-style of the actor or the writer. He also feels ("Return to Tipasa," 1955) that it is possible for every man who gives himself fully to the sun, the earth, the elements, to become like one of the simple Algerians, primitively and sensually relating to life as it occurs. An example of this optimistic species of existentialism is noted in the following speech:

> I leave Sisyphus at the foot of the mountain! One always finds one's burden again. But Sisyphus teaches the higher fidelity that negates the gods and raises rocks. He too concluded that all is well. This universe henceforth without a master seems to him neither sterile nor futile. Each atom of that stone, each mineral flake of that night-filled mountain, in itself forms a world. The struggle itself toward the heights is enough to fill a man's heart. One must imagine Sisyphus happy.

This kind of positive thrust, despite Camus' taking what many call an unjustified intellectual leap, provides a natural connection with the philosophical backdrop against which humanistic psychologists would test other main forces in psychology, psychoanalysis, and behaviorism. Camus' later works remind us of the early writings of Viktor Frankl, who, discussing his concentration camp experiences (1959), also came to the ultimate conclusion that man can live positively, opt for positive or constructive choices, and discover the meaning of his own life, even in the face of death and amid the horrors of an existence with no semblance of "justice."

This short historical survey into the origins of humanistic and existential thinking demonstrates two factors common to today's movement of humanism in the sciences: (1) criticism of rigid methodology and of confining study to certain prescribed areas and patterns, and (2) concentration on man experiencing his existence.

C. The dual impact of humanism

What is the significance of humanistic psychology's development away from the mainstream of other major schools? We have indicated that the new school adopted two philosophical approaches to man: humanism and existentialism. The humanistic psychologist wanted to retain his image of man while systematically studying the human being. His metatheoretical position required a revolutionary attitude toward science as a whole and toward his participation in it. In 1966 Maslow described the humanistic psychologist's turning away from the rigid convention of "normal science" (Kuhn, 1962) toward innovative explorations of man which might be classified as more Eastern than Western, since they acknowledge the constant change in man and in social systems and emphasize flux rather than stasis. Humanists thus emphasize the image of man as active and positive, as experiencing his existence. This perspective differs considerably from the more reactive models of the Freudians and psychoanalysts.

The impact of existentialism on this school is significant in defining the role of experience. Nietzsche and Kierkegaard are understood only superficially if considered as theorists per se. The fact of their visceral existence—that they observed life as they lived it, free from need to protest their objectivity—is essential if we are to bridge the gap between detached comprehension of their message and personal connection with their fear and trembling, their ecstasies and despairs.

Thus humanistic psychology is revolutionary in that (1) it presents a positive model of man, and (2) its proponents, admitting their own beingness, believe that life is to be lived subjectively, as it takes place. Humanistic psychologists are human beings first and scientists second. Even in the moment of observation they do not claim to be "objective." They are intent on the discovery of methods within the highly subjective interchange of a relationship which will garner "personal knowledge" of another human being (Polanyi, 1958). These deviations from scientific tradition, combined with awareness of limitations as observer and interpreter of human behavior, have made the humanistic psychologist vulnerable. However, it is this very vulnerability which he attempts to maintain, for, as he believes in the new model of man as one who experiences, so must he experience. He observes Sisyphus forever pushing his rock up the mountain and recognizes himself.

3

Theoretical concepts

In August 1970 the First International Congress of Humanistic Psychology convened at the New University of Amsterdam. Representatives from many countries met to "pool" their ideas and their work, hoping thereby to provide the groundwork for further organization and discourse. A central purpose of this conference was to consolidate the theoretical constructs which had been formulated during the short life of humanistic psychology. Charlotte Bühler, as President of the Congress, attempted to work these concepts into a systematic, coherent whole. It was believed then and is still held that these theoretical formulations are as basic to the continuation and fruition of this new school as are the more publicized experiential factors. This chapter presents much of the material offered by Bühler in Amsterdam and includes further elaborations by both authors of this book on the theoretical problems involved in studying the human organism as a whole. We believe that the main task confronting humanistic psychologists today is to present a logical thesis which justifies a humanistic science of man.

Chapter 3 is an extension of the following article: Bühler, C., "Basic theoretical concepts of humanistic psychology," *American Psychologist,* 1971, **26,** 378–386. Copyright 1971 by the American Psychological Association and reproduced by permission.

A. The whole person as model

One tenet of humanistic psychology that is generally agreed upon is that we must strive to study and understand the *person as a whole.* Structural experimental psychology has never succeeded in this task; neither has American behaviorism. Among European systems, Gestalt psychology accomplished the most cogent concept of the whole individual. But most of the Gestaltists' actual research was concerned with the perceived more than the acting whole. The total action-perception process was more a subject of speculation than of knowledge. Psychoanalysts had a concept of the person as a whole, but, as mentioned before, their theory of healthy persons' functioning was unconvincing to many, especially with respect to their goals. In fact, some analysts ridiculed the idea that a "healthy" person could be found.

Attempts to construct the total person out of details gathered from experiments and from observations of specific functions and behaviors have been prevalent until recently. Furthermore, according to the rules of modern science, the individual was studied as a member of a group; the study of a single individual was not considered a proper scientific goal.

Attempts to depart from this approach and from science as a model were made earlier, notably by Wilhelm Dilthey, a German historian, and Eduard Spranger, a German educational psychologist. These men attempted to establish the method of understanding rather than explaining as the only suitable means to know a person as a whole individual. Spranger also emphasized the concept of values as fundamentally important to understanding humans. Dilthey, Spranger, Brentano, and Husserl laid the groundwork for the *methodology* of what they termed *idiographic* in contrast to *nomothetic* sciences, the study of individuals apart from groups. They worked out the difference between "casual processes" and "meaningful relations." "Understanding," says Dilthey, "is the rediscovery of the I in the Thou" (1961, p. 67). But, as Allport (1942) pointed out, the idiographic method has serious validation problems.

Michael Polanyi (1958), with great erudition, discussed the fundamental differences between a machine and a person and the different methods of study applicable to each. He also demonstrated the objectivity and thus scientific justification for what he calls research by way of "participating experience," which naturally becomes a "subjective" procedure. However, he believes that personal participation does not necessarily make our understanding subjective. "Comprehension," on the basis of personal participation, he says, "is neither an arbitrary act nor a passive experience, but a responsible act claiming universal validity."

Floyd Matson, considering this same question, discusses "understanding of personal experience in its complementary wholeness" (1964). He also quotes the psychiatrist Viktor von Weizsäcker, who combines "understanding" of the person with objective treatments and techniques. In Weizsäcker's system of "medical anthropology," all objective diagnoses and specifications are rendered secondary to the task of comprehending the patient as a whole person, a unique and irreducible subject. On the basis of this "inclusive" understanding, Weizsäcker believes, the complementary tasks of objective treatment and technique may proceed without hazarding a fragmentation of the person which will destroy his identity.

Weizsäcker implies that it is possible to handle the main problem in successfully studying a person—that is, to combine findings in terms of objective data with what Polanyi calls "personal knowledge" rather than "subjective understanding."

In his *Psychology of Science* (1966) Maslow wrote: "The basic coin in the realm of knowing is direct, intimate, experiential knowing" (p. 46) and "There is no substitute for experience, none at all" (p. 45). "I must approach a person as an individual, unique and peculiar, as the sole member of his class" (p. 10).

This approach raises serious problems regarding *predictability,* one of the most important criteria of scientific reliability. It is a tricky problem, because in certain respects prediction of human action is possible, although it also may fail completely.

Even a behavior therapist such as Aubrey J. Yates, in his recent book *Behavior Therapy* (1970), calls it a "self-deception" to assume that the behavior-therapy approach has been, or can be, validated in terms of predictability. He declares: "(a) There are presently no standard techniques of behavior therapy available, nor are there likely to be in the foreseeable future. (b) Each abnormality of behavior represents a new problem so that each patient must be considered a subject of experimental investigation in his own right" (p. 380). This makes Aubrey sound like a humanist!

Another behaviorist, Mischel (1968), presents an excellent review of the problems implicit in personality assessment. The inability to evaluate with validity and reliability is skillfully discussed by this author. He concludes that personality variables in human states are highly complex, transient, and situation-specific. They defy the scientist's zeal to explain and predict, for it is often impossible to select the relevant variables. Even with accurate focus, uncontrolled variation and experimenter effect may influence the measurement.

The purpose of psychology is to understand the individual as a whole. Scientific psychology, beginning with Wilhelm Wundt (1832–1920), used physics and chemistry, then well-established sciences, as models. Wundt taught that we should study the elements of consciousness which can be accounted for quantitatively (sensations, images, feelings). He experimented with isolated reactions to stimuli and with memory, since responses to each are indicated by immediate verbal report. By this means he hoped eventually to acquire knowledge of the whole individual.

But Wundt must have recognized that this goal would never be reached. Concurrent with his exact experiments of sensory reactions to stimuli, he wrote a treatise on ethnopsychology, a study of people which was anything but exact or even generally well documented according to present values of anthropological and ethnological study. Nevertheless he became a world authority and had followers everywhere. Many of his students had established their own laboratories in Europe and the United States by the end of the nineteenth century.

In Russia in 1902 Ivan Pavlov introduced the study of conditioned reflexes. The American John Watson (1878–1958) was also a student of conditioned responses, or reflexes. Some of his ideas are extended in modern American behavior psychology and behavior psychotherapy.

In Germany, where Wundt's reign had been supreme, opposition arose in 1903, first in the Würzburg school of thought processes and then in the school of Gestalt psychology.

The Würzburg school under Oswald Külpe, with Ach, Dürr, Watt, Messer, K. Bühler, and later Selz as leading figures, demonstrated that thought processes are not simply reactions to sensory stimuli but can be "spontaneous"—perhaps "creative" (in modern terms)—and that quantitative studies of them are impossible and irrelevant. Karl Bühler had the courage to attack Wundt in an article which evoked Wundt's ire but which was admired by many. He demonstrated further that thought processes and perception function in a way not easily quantified and explained only superficially as mere reactions to external stimuli.

Investigating the concept of original *Gestaltqualität*—translated roughly as "the quality conferred by a pattern"—Bühler made an experimental study of the perception of rectangles (1913). In hundreds of systematic experiments with rectangles of different sizes, he proved that all his subjects could instantly recognize a rectangle no matter the shape and without reducing or breaking down their perception, as in the Wundt experiments.

Meanwhile, Kurt Koffka, Max Wertheimer, and especially Wolfgang Köhler concentrated on the problem of Gestalt perception, a process differing from reactions to single stimuli. They were interested in the *dynamics,* those forces producing Gestalt perception. Wertheimer studied the perception of moving objects, while Köhler developed a theory of the physical brain processes underlying Gestalt perception.

Kurt Lewin, the youngest of the Gestaltists and Köhler's student, turned from theories concerning physical processes to studies of mental and emotional dynamics involved in response to awards, punishments, and aspirations. He coined the term *aspiration level.* He describes a child looking through a shop window at some candy; the child is greatly attracted but also inhibited in his impulse to get what he desires. And herein lies the great limitation of Lewinian psychology: his descriptions of behavior do not explain the forces which motivate them, because he neither accepts nor replaces the Freudian theory of motivation. He describes his psychology as topological, which indicates that it is more descriptive than analytic.

A trend in the direction of humanistic psychological thinking was started by the neurologist Kurt Goldstein (1939), who developed and demonstrated a completely new dynamic principle: the healthy individual's increasing need for self-actualization, which he believed to be a basic motive as well as goal of life. Maslow (1954) agreed, rejecting the Freudian motivational principles to which he had adhered previously.

The single-case study

Allen (1970b) assembled data to justify the validity of the single-case study, a method frequently denigrated by many psychologists. She demonstrated the relevance of this methodology for the clinician and for the humanistically oriented psychologist. American psychology has traditionally rejected this concept. The nomothetic orientation stems from loyalty to the Law of Large Numbers. It claims that research involving the individual is too expensive and impractical to be warranted, since it usually does not lead to results applicable to large groups. This insistence, in its extreme, advocates that only hypothesis-testing with groups qualifies as scientific procedure for the psychologist. According to Shontz (1965), it has led to many instances wherein the researcher has failed to realize the efficacy and suitability of the $N=1$—that is, the single-case study—in a particular instance.

Is there a place for the single-case study in contemporary behavioral research? *If* the single case or representative case has utility, what are its main assets and when can we appropriately use it?

Another common misconception is that the single-case model is used only to explore *individual differences.* But Dukes (1965), in his historical review of this area, illustrated that, of 264 studies made (1939–1963) which followed this method, a wide range of psychological areas used such a design. Only 30 percent of the studies involved were idiographically oriented. Most of the studies referred to were concerned with "treating the individual as a *universe of responses* and applying traditionally nomothetic techniques to describe and predict individual behavior" (italics ours). The pioneer studies of Ebbinghaus (1885), who used himself as his sole subject in performing tasks of verbal retention, and the original baby studies of Charlotte Bühler (1927) operated under the assumption that there are many situations in which the individual is not deviant from the target population and is therefore a representative case. Utilization of individual study, when it *is* representational, is most appropriate as part of the deductive process in research (Shontz, 1965), rather than in the inductive, more conventional use of hypothesis-testing with groups.

In his excellent review of $N=1$ research, Dukes also notes:

"In actual practice . . . the two orientations—toward uniqueness or generality—are more a matter of degree than of mutual exclusion, with the result that in the literature surveyed, purely idiographic research is extremely rare" (p. 76).

There is also a statistical and methodological rationale for the $N=1$ case study. Shontz hypothesizes that common misconceptions regarding limitations of the representative case study and the single-case study have often issued out of naïveté concerning methodological procedures. Here Shontz emphasizes the necessity for familiarizing ourselves with that design-model appropriate to the questions we desire to answer as scientists.

In the representative case study, for instance, Shontz indicates that many of the conventions operative in traditional research will be modified. Standard randomization procedures, for example, cannot be utilized in the choice of subjects, for individuals are well known previous to the study. How, then, do advocates of single-case designs handle the problem of possible experimenter bias if their subjects *are* well known? Both Shontz and Chassan (1960) admit to inherent problems but claim that these possible limitations are compensated for by the opportunity for intensive study of the individual, which affords information not given by research using faceless subjects. Chassan discusses in detail the value of intensive as opposed to extensive studies.

Both Chassan and Shontz emphasize two major advantages of $N=1$ research: (1) the opportunity to vary systematically all pertinent levels of the independent variable in focus and (2) the opportunity to treat the experimenter variable as part of the investigation, systematically varying different experimenters and different experiment behaviors with the same subject. This sort of procedure is based on the assumption of *intrasubject* variability (Chassan, 1960), a foil to the hard-core researcher and an emphasis of the humanistically oriented scientist. Frequent observations of the same individual under varieties of situations provide more accurate results than do "end-point observations over a relatively large number of patients" (Shontz, 1965). As for possible bias, Shontz advises that, as with any research, utmost care must be taken that data be strong in "immediacy, objectivity, and relevance." Again, it must be stressed that, although we can scientifically justify research with individuals, this does not mean that casual observation and introspection qualify as research.

McNemar (1940) offers a statistician's judgment on the utility of the single-case study: "The statistician who fails to see that important generalization from research on a single case can ever be acceptable, is on a par with the experimentalist who fails to appreciate the fact that some problems can never be solved without resort to numbers" (p. 361).

Chassan (1960) offers a skillful example of this lack of vision and "scientific behavior" in demonstrating that standard hypothesis-testing for significance may actually result in an incorrect conclusion regarding the results of studies in the clinical setting with small groups. This is true because of the extremely high success-to-failure ratio required when one deals with small groups —that is, there are few degrees of freedom. Inappropriate application of this conventional model in certain settings has, claims Chassan, doubtlessly led to many a lead being lost, to many a valid hypothesis being forsaken. The fact that a difference has been observed is often forgotten. In the instance of research with small groups, we are frankly able neither to disprove the null hypothesis (as differences were actually observed between groups of subjects) nor to support our research hypothesis (as the required level of significance has not been attained). Chassan offers as an alternative the intensive study of one individual. This technique enables us to make many observations and determine whether or not a real effect exists (an effect due to our treatment rather than to chance).

> From the point of view of statistical inference per se the intensive single-case study can be considered as providing data sampled from a statistical distribution or population defined by the set of particular parameters or characteristics of the patient under study ... one's expectations of a similarity of result depend simply on the assumption that this second patient is representative of a population to that of the design patient to permit inferences from the one to the other (1960, p. 179).

In other words, with proper use of this design, generalization can be made to those subjects represented by the design subject.

Duke concludes that statistically the $N=1$ case is justified in several situations: (1) when uniqueness is obvious—that is, when one subject exhausts a certain population (this is absolute idiopathy and would be true in studying any human organism as a holistic entity); (2) when complete population generality exists (intersubject variability is so low that it does not matter which subject we select for our measurement); (3) in the case of an intensive study of an "ideal" or "typical" or "representative" case; (4) when the findings of the study end in *dis*proving an asserted or assumed universal relationship (herein, Dukes indicates that our single study has proved to be a critical study of a hypothesis); (5) when chances to observe a particular kind of case are limited (this would justify the focusing of research resources on an individual and would overcompensate for customary practical considerations).

Shontz concludes his justification for the "representative case" by stating:

> The intensive test of a theoretical proposition in an individual case, providing it is properly done, is far more rigorous and demanding than the survey of a thousand people with questionnaires that ask how they feel about insects and about their mothers. . . . Each individual, as an individual, constitutes one full and complete test of the universal proposition (1965, p. 252).

Considerations of open-systems theory

The importance of open-systems theory to the study of the person as a whole has been stressed by Allen (1970c) with the following argument.

The growing popularity of considering the human organism as an *open system* is largely due to the pioneer work of L. von Bertalanffy, who as early as 1940 proposed this conceptual framework of systems as applicable and utilitarian across the scientific disciplines. G. Allport (1960) describes a "system" as "any complex of elements in mutual interaction." In speaking of a closed system, he writes of elements self-contained, a system "that admits no matter from outside itself . . . (and) has no restorative properties and no transactions with its environment."

Let us illustrate how an organism interacts with various other systems. These systems could be depicted as sets of circles, some overlapping, some capable of changing the degree of overlap (thereby changing the state of interaction), and some fluctuating in interrelationship in time. The human organism, for instance, moves in and out of various behavioral settings (or fields, which are themselves systems), and this organism, which is itself a system, may interact with various other systems simultaneously. (It should be noted that there can be more than one interaction with one field or environment at any given moment.) Von Bertalanffy contrasts this species of conception to that of the closed system, stating: "The open system continually gives up matter to the outer world and takes in matter from it, but (it) maintains itself in this continuous exchange in a steady-state, or approaches such steady-states in its variations over time" (1951).

Is this steady-state that which we term *homeostasis?* In "General Systems Theory" (1966) von Bertalanffy revises earlier formulations and clarifies his notion of steady-state: "a distance from true equilibrium." Also emphasized as distinctly human is the *tendency toward order and ordering.* The traditional biologistic or materialistic thesis holds that *all* organic matter has a tendency to move toward *entropy* or disorganization. As this is not true for the human organism, von Bertalanffy cautions behaviorists that they must always be prepared for responses which he terms "highly statistically improbable"—certain acts characterized by maintenance of order and organization that are known to be clearly nonsupportive of the above "universal law." One of our tenets in humanistic psychology is that the human being tends toward higher degrees of order over the course of his life, allowing for temporary disorders in the process. This is particularly characteristic of the *human adaptation process.*

To extend further upon his conception of the steady-state as different from that of true equilibrium, von Bertalanffy (1968) believes that, within such periods, the human organism is still capable "of doing work." This frees us from more static concepts of balance or homeostasis and allows us to consider certain behaviors which in themselves seem to be acts causing "disequilibrium" to the organism. Herein we specifically refer to movements of the organism toward his environment, with no seeming physical stimulation from that environment, at a time when apparently he felt no drive state, no need frustration, no state of tension. Reporting on studies of the infant in his first year of life, C. Bühler (1930) remarked that, when fed, rested, and in a familiar environment, the baby often enjoys certain acts of self-stimulation such as finger play. Earlier, K. Bühler (1918) had viewed similar acts as indicative of a pleasure function. C. Bühler (1954) commented that such outward-striving behaviors defy the simple drive-reduction explanations and that "there is a pleasure in the stimulating process, not only in its reduction." She insisted on a dual-factor theory which would consider these expansive tendencies and indicated that such acts might later fit into a context of "adaptation, positive anticipation, and vigilance." Certainly the data we now possess from studies dealing with either total or partial sensory deprivation (Zubek, 1969) are related to this consideration. C. Bühler stated (1954) that the organism has "a desire to operate within and master an environment which, if successfully coped with, can at a given moment be a 'positive reality as well as negatively inhibiting' as Freud would have it." Beyond the artificial constructs of sensory-deprivation experiments, activities such as exploration, curiosity, and creativity support the notion of a positive reality principle and continue to defy drive-reduction theorists.

Allport (1960) and von Bertalanffy (1968) allude to "growth motives" in the human organism, equating such motives with the tendency to higher degrees of organization. We would prefer to speak of a tendency to conditions of more complex order. Many areas of psychological research attest to findings which would support the credence of such concepts. Numerous studies in stress reactions and coping strategies demonstrate that the human organism gears himself for the reduction of tension not only at the present moment, but in anticipation of events to come (Fenz & Epstein, 1969; Goldstein & Adams, 1967, 1969). C. Bühler (1954) discusses the infant's subconscious anticipation of reality as a place where he can do something.

If one insists on fidelity to a *learning-theory* framework, one could interpret such gradually developed sets of behaviors as learning to adapt. But we suggest that these complicated patterns of behavior are supportive of our own humanistic orientation.

In consolidating criteria for an open system, Allport formulates four principles which he deems essential to this species of system:

1. There must be both an intake and an output of matter and energy.

2. Steady-states are achieved and maintained so that the intru-
   sion of outer energy will not seriously disrupt internal form
   and order.
3. There is generally an increase of order over time, owing to an
   increase in complexity and differentiation of parts.
4. At least in the human organism, there is not simply intake
   and output of matter and energy but extensive transitional
   commerce with the environment.

Allport states that the stimulus-response models of the
strict behaviorists accept the first two criteria. But with emphasis
on "stability rather than growth, permanence rather than change,"
these more rudimentary and reductionistically insistent theories
are "biologistic" in orientation. Advocates of open-systems theory
are, because of their emphasis on organism-environment interaction, committed to what Allport termed "tension-enhancement as
well as tension-reduction, proaction as well as reaction." Methodologically, these factors clearly demonstrate measurement problems which point in the direction of the phenomenological orientation to behavior.

We are aware that the nature of the open-systems framework threatens our conventional "need to quantify." We are led
into considerations of certain behavioral acts or sequences difficult
to assess probabilistically. Also, because of continuously changing
situations wherein the organism as open system moves from one
or more behavioral settings to others, we are also required to
recognize the need for $N=1$ studies—that is, studies of one individual, which if sometimes primitive and lacking in statistical
elegance are nevertheless appropriate to this framework.

The course of human life as a whole

Understanding a human being as a whole requires and
implies the knowledge of his whole life history. It is a strange
contradiction that in psychiatric practice it was always considered
proper procedure to take a patient's history but that, on the other
hand, in the psychiatric treatment the patient was rarely related
to the course of life as a whole. Neither psychology nor psychiatry
has yet concerned itself much with life-cycle studies. In 1933
C. Bühler attempted to stress such studies as a starting point

necessary to the understanding of human life. But life-cycle studies until now have been few, largely due to the methodological problems involved in including and organizing the bulk of material necessary.

One of the basic questions in this approach, whether we are using biographies or case histories, is the point of view from which they are presented and the technique applied in the organization of the data. As humanistic psychologists, we are faced with the same problem we mentioned with respect to understanding the person as a whole: that of devising a method to report objective data of the life history together with an account of the person's inner attitudes and responses to events in his own life. C. Bühler attempted this in her first sketch of biographical studies (1933), in which presentation of the sequence of events was given concurrently with the sequences of the person's inner experiences and production. She related the whole to what she regarded as an underlying biological scheme, codetermining the order of events, experiences, and products. She does in no way, however, mean to reduce psychological development to a strictly biologistic or mechanical level. In particular, she stresses interaction with the environment and the importance of the individual self, which later came to be emphasized in open-systems theory.

In the meantime other approaches were made, one from the viewpoint of *psychoanalysis,* in its older and classical, as well as its more recent *ego-psychological,* versions. Erik Erikson (1959) is an outstanding representative of this method. Erikson studied individual lives in order to find central concerns, whereas Freud and his earlier followers were chiefly interested in the history of a person's emotional illness.

As far as other biographical studies are concerned, their emphasis and orientation concern personality factors (in which Henry A. Murray had been interested since 1938), sociological and environmental conditionings of the individual (which Havighurst had investigated on a large scale since the middle 1940s), and statistical-behavioristic investigations (which Pressey and Kuhlen first applied mostly to groups). A recent book of H. Thomae (1968) also uses behavior statistics in addition to interview material.

These studies related either not at all or very little to that question which is of central importance to the humanistic psychologist: whether we can or cannot assume that human life is lived by man—if not by all—with a definite purpose directed toward a personal endgoal.

The main controversy in this matter, we believe, centers around another question: can we conceive of a person's life as centralized in some core, or is such a unity fictitious, hypothetical, and the result of an optimistic interpretation? Or is it, as some say, reductionistic? Another controversial point is to what degree, if at all, the development of a person during his life history is codetermined by biological processes. Third and less stringent is the question of whether we should in fact see an individual's life history in a sequence of phases and, if so, how these are to be determined.

We believe that, in studying a healthy person's existence, it has a core which may be unconscious and not the source or the system of referral for his actions. But still we find that it is almost always traceable, and the development has some relationship to biological processes. We also can apply a schematic organization of the material in phases, which is helpful in providing an overview of the data.

A humanistic model of psychosocial development

Charles Hampden-Turner (1970) brings a humanistic orientation to the task of model building. He investigates rebellion, growth, and regression in training groups. He reports more than 200 studies dealing with social structures, corporate radicalism, and conservative and radical issues in American politics.

In Hampden-Turner's review of Rokeach's *The Open and the Closed Mind* (Rokeach, 1960), the dogmatism of the old communist Left and that of the extreme Right appear the same. Each is high in anomie, conventionality, and "classical Conservatism." Conservatives advocate the suppression of inner feelings, while the developmental New Left are more flexible, take genuine risk, and are convinced that, because their personal expression is authentically true to the human condition, others somewhere will appreciate its basic humanity.

Hampden-Turner includes a discussion of student radicals, especially middle-class elements of the New Left, and cites many findings about student activists in various American colleges. In the Rhode Island School of Design, highly creative students were in favor of a sane nuclear policy; in four colleges 43 percent of protesters against Vietnam were in the top range of academic excellence; in Chicago student activists were highly influenced by existentialism and humanism. No evidence was found in the investigation that "the 'worst elements' are most active and duping well-meaning moderates" (1970, p. 362).

To the question "Why now this unrest?" Hampden-Turner replies that these students are vehemently protesting "the threatened end of their development as people," since persons in high places within the university are seen as hand in glove with corporate and political interests.

In this very thorough piece of research, Hampden-Turner provides a sound argument for the humanistic model of man. He patterns his personality model from the writings of humanistic psychologists, primarily Maslow. Hampden-Turner unites Maslow's qualities of self-actualizing persons with Kohlberg's (1969) six stages of moral development. Kohlberg's six stages are as follows:

Stages of Development*

Stage 1. Obedience and punishment orientation, egocentric deference to superior power or prestige, or a trouble-avoiding set. Objective responsibility.
Stage 2. Instrumental Relativists (IR). Naively egoistic orientation: Right Action is that instrumentally satisfying the self's needs and occasionally others'. Awareness of relativism of value to each actor's needs and perspective. Naive egalitarianism and orientation to exchange and reciprocity.
Stage 3. Personal Concordance (PC). Good-boy orientation. Orientation to approval and to pleasing and helping others. Conformity to stereotypical images of majority or natural role behavior and judgment by intentions.
Stage 4. Law and Order (LO). Authority and social-order maintaining orientation. Orientation to "doing duty" and to showing respect for authority and maintaining the

*From L. Kohlberg, "Stage and Sequence: The Cognitive Developmental Approach to Socialization." In A. Croslin (Ed.), *Handbook of Socialization Theory and Research,* pp. 120–121. New York: Rand-McNally, 1969. Reprinted by permission.

given social order for its own sake. Regard for earned expectations of others.

Stage 5. Social Contract (SC). Contractual legalistic orientation. Recognition of an arbitrary element or starting point in rules or expectations for the sake of agreement. Duty defined in terms of contract, general avoidance of violations of the will or rights of others, and majority will and welfare.

Stage 6. Individual Principles (IP). Conscience or principle orientation. Orientation not only to actually ordained social rules but to principles of choice involving appeal to logical universality and consistency. Orientation to conscience as a directing agent and to mutual respect and trust.

The self-actualized individual, according to Hampden-Turner, is the person who is capable of making the highest form of moral judgment—that judgment based on principle and conscience. Such a person is one:

a. Whose *perception* was courageous enough to focus upon the range of the dilemmas, and was accurate enough in gauging the needs of the other to regard this specific judgment as superior to existing laws and contracts which conflicted with it.

b. Whose *identity* was strong enough to override the role expectations thrust upon him by the culture (Stage 3).

c-d. Whose *competence* at authentic *investing* was great enough to communicate and to act upon the principle he saw despite the likelihood of conflict and opposition.

e. Who would *risk suspending* social contracts (Stage 5), laws (Stage 4), role-expectations (Stage 3), and *risk* personal inconvenience (Stage 2) and punishment (Stage 1) in order to express a better principle than custom enshrined.

f. Who would *bridge the distance* created between himself and others, consequent upon his breaking of laws and conventions at stages 3 to 5.

g. Whose selected principle is so well chosen and communicated that it calls forth a *confirming* response in others, and *transcends* not only the communicator himself but previous contracts, laws, and role expectations (stages 3 to 5).

h. Whose selected principle is capable of becoming a new social contract (Stage 5) and later a new law (Stage 4) and a role-model (Stage 3). He would thereby eventually reconcile the opposites between law and conscience and through a dialectic between the two achieve a *higher synergy* of justice and universalized principles.

i. Whose experience of moral choice and action would increase
his *complex integration* of the principles of conscience.*

Kohlberg's study leads Hampden-Turner to some important conclusions regarding rebels. Rebellion can occur at either of
two stages, the highly moral or the premoral. This makes it difficult to distinguish in any revolutionary movement those who act
with responsibility and insight from those who are simply destructive.

Youth is not a necessary factor in constructive rebellion.
Personality variables are more important than age variables in
establishing new ways of being.

Some people cannot rebel. Kohlberg reports a drastic experiment, devised by Stanley Milgram (1961) at Yale University,
to demonstrate the inability of many people to break away from
authoritarian structure. In this experiment subjects were ordered
to administer electric shock to other subjects (who were in fact
stooges). Obeying the commands of the experimenters in authority, they raised the voltage even beyond the blatantly marked
danger point on the equipment. Very few of the subjects refused
the directions of the experimenters, even though they thought
they were inflicting pain on others. Many persons have made a
connection between these results and conditions of mass genocide,
such as in the Nazi period.

Hampden-Turner's radical man would have been able to
risk defying authority for his belief in the principle of human life.
His humanistic commitment would have required him to act out
of conscience, refusing to comply with orders antagonistic to his
value system. Today's *constructive* radical *can* pit himself against
the Establishment to work for that reform which his conscience
dictates.

Another segment of our society that might be said to
exemplify the Hampden Turner model is the new breed of volun
teer in all branches of life. The United States has produced much
volunteer activity, both financial and personal. Joyce E. Pereira
(1947) and Eduard Lindeman (1921) describe the history of this
movement. Great Britain, too, has a tradition of volunteers. Ger-

aldine M. Aves' book *The Volunteer Worker in the Social Services* (1970) describes the contemporary role of the volunteer, stressing that, through his services, the volunteer establishes for himself new opportunities for self-realization. In contrast with past focus on the voluntary organization, the new emphasis is on the volunteer himself.

In a movement complementary to that of the activists who take reforms into their own hands, these volunteers tackle problem areas where insufficient public or private assistance is available. They have attempted to lessen the squalor in Watts; they have founded the Head-Start movement, teaching disadvantaged children and their families; they have made themselves in a wide network of activities to be "their brothers' keepers."

Eva Schindler-Rainman and Ronald Lippitt, in a most enlightening volume called *The Volunteer Community* (1971), described the human services that volunteers provide these days in "classroom teaching, medical service, child care activities, social work services, tutoring, and many other areas of community activity" (p. 38). Schindler-Rainman and Lippitt also enumerate many other areas that would profit from volunteer activities.

The important factor here is what these volunteers derive for themselves in the act of helping. Perhaps their feelings are engendered partially out of knowledge of the mutual effort required to rebuild our society in a time of crisis. A positive aspect of the encounter-group movement has been its demonstration of this reconstruction in microcosm.

At such a time, when old methods for dealing with life problems seem inappropriate, when old values are under fire, when *all* people seek new ways to cope with human life as a whole, we understand the widespread appeal of a humanistically oriented model of man. No psychology as such can provide a philosophy for all men, but humanistic psychology is perhaps in a better position to help the individual toward this goal, since it focuses specifically on the discovery of principles which have proved constructive in building and maintaining meaningful lives and because it allows room for each individual to grasp those principles and those individual potentialities most useful to him in the rebuilding of his own life.

This is what most of us have been seeking—if not a "whole new philosophy," then at least some general principles which, given our own particular requirements for satisfaction, will help us to experience personal meaning in our lives, despite the fact that the meaning of life itself may elude us.

B. The perspective of the humanistic psychologist

As mentioned in the previous chapter, although the primary concern of the humanistic psychologist has been to present a theoretical model of man as positive, active, and purposive, a second concern is his own involvement with the life experience itself. He does not stand apart aloof, introspective, and hypothesizing. He emphasizes full participation in life and includes himself as a participant. He enters scientific endeavors and therapeutic relationships as a person. The following section discusses the humanistic psychologist's awareness of *intentional* and *creative* aspects of the human being.

Human existence and intentionality

The problem of understanding the person as an entirety in the whole course of his life has brought humanistic psychology into close relationship with existentialism—or, more precisely, existential considerations form the underlying philosophical basis of humanistic psychology. The experience of human existence is an essential basis for humanistic concept formation. Rollo May (1958) has shown the relevance of existentialism to humanistic psychology as well as to humanistic psychotherapy. The essential goal of the humanistic psychotherapist is to help the person experience his existence as real.

Experiencing the reality of one's existence can occur in various ways. The peak experience described by Maslow actually represents the peak of awareness. Flashes of insight and of understanding may offer the elating experience of seizing upon true reality.

To us the strongest path appears to be the reality experience of intentionality, this core of a person's self and of his motivation. We refer to Rollo May's (1969) lucid discussion of the complexity of the concept of intentionality. This concept, first introduced into psychology by Franz Brentano, combines a *cognitive* with a *conative* aspect. Intentionality implies both a person's focusing on a subject which means something to him and his directing himself toward that subject. May quotes Husserl's statement "Meaning is an intention of the mind," including both the meaning and the act, the moving toward something. "Meaning," concludes May, "has within it a commitment," and *"cognition, or knowing, and conation, or willing, then go together"* (p. 230).

Of fundamental importance is May's application of this insight to the process of psychotherapy. He shows how a patient's ability to *see* his problem develops only to the degree that he is able to *do* something about it. He says: "The patient cannot permit himself to perceive the trauma until he is ready to take a stand toward it. What goes on is a curious inner conversation with ourselves, 'I know I will be able to see this later on, but I cannot see it now.' This is simply a way of saying, 'I know it is true, but I cannot yet permit myself to see it.'" (pp. 231–232). In this connection he quotes Merleau-Ponty (1964): "Every intention is an attention, and attention is I-can." Therefore we are unable to give attention to something until we are able in some way to experience an "I-can" with regard to it.

What happens in this process is "a change in the patient's relation to his world, generally by way of his increased capacity to trust the therapist and, accordingly, himself" (1969, p. 232). The recovery of memory is also seen by May as a function of intentionality. Memory is like perception in this regard; the patient cannot remember something until he is ready to take some stand toward it. "Recovery of childhood memories," Franz Alexander put it, "is not the cause but the result of analysis" (May, 1969, p. 232).

May conceives of intentionality as underlying both conscious and unconscious intentions. It refers to a state of being and involves, to a greater or lesser degree, the totality of the person's orientation to the world at that time.

The *self as the central core of the person* is, we believe, a generally accepted concept of humanistic psychologists. It differs from the psychoanalytic concept of the self as object—that is, as being built up and representing a whole only in the reflecting person's mind. This innermost self, or "core system," is the origin for the individual's goal setting. The more modern view is the humanistic one, wherein the self is seen as *subject.*

Motivation, goal setting, and creativity

One of the main points of the humanistic psychologist's new orientation is his concept of the healthy person's *endgoal* in life. Kurt Goldstein (1939) and C. Bühler (1933) criticized the psychoanalytic concept of *homeostasis* as endgoal. Goldstein showed convincingly that homeostasis becomes a goal only in sickness. Bühler discussed homeostasis as a transitory state from which the healthy human being moves actively outward toward fulfilling accomplishments. Among humanistic psychologists, the most widespread theory is that of the endgoal of self-realization, first suggested by Karen Horney (1950) and Erich Fromm (1941), or self-actualization, suggested by Kurt Goldstein (1939) and Abraham Maslow (1954). Some authors prefer to emphasize other characteristics of this process of development. Carl Rogers speaks of it as a growth process in which potentialities are brought to realization. C. Bühler (1962) emphasizes, as does Von Bertalanffy (1966), that essential to the self-realization process is the experience of bringing *values* to materialization. Viktor Frankl (1969) asserts that human existence is self-transcending and that the human goal lies in fulfillment of a personal meaning.

The common denominator of these concepts is that all humanistic psychologists see the goal of life as that of using it to accomplish something in which one believes. From this they expect a *fulfillment* toward which people direct themselves (C. Bühler, 1933).

This does not, of course, necessarily mean that everybody pursues this endgoal consistently and coherently. Probably nobody does so. It is not possible to go through life without experiencing interruptions or side-trackings from long-term, ultimate goals. Many people seem to live without direction; they may squander themselves in the pursuit of immediate pleasures or short-term satisfactions. Also, when illness or failures defeat a person, or when decline is experienced with fear of its outcome, the endgoal of self-realization and of fulfillment may become lost. In all these negative circumstances, the wish for easing of condi-

tions is foremost. Thus homeostatic tendencies prevail in incapaci-
tating sickness, as Goldstein saw in 1939. And probably no one is
entirely free from the struggle between what Maslow (1956) calls
growth motivation and *deficiency* motivation. This is where problems and conflicts, anxiety, and guilt are confronted by necessity.
The conceptual understanding of these motivational experiences
belongs to the main body of humanistic psychology's still unresolved problems.

Freud, who discovered the process of repression of conflicts and guilts into the unconscious, theorized that all human
conflicts result from the clash of an individual's wishes with reality's obstacles and society's demands. He viewed the workings of
conscience in the guilt feelings that society via the parents instilled
in the mind of the child set on wish-fulfillment.

Humanistic psychology points to a personal guilt aside
from socially conditioned guilt feelings. Self-guilt may arise in an
individual who squanders his life, failing to fulfill or develop his
own best potentials—who does not do what he believes he should.
Humanistic psychologists feel that this failing of one's own self is
a more crucial aspect of self-condemnation than is the guilt in-
duced by socially unacceptable actions.

May (1969) attempts a new approach to a solution of this
problem. He tries to introduce *will* in a newly defined manner,
showing it in opposition to, as well as in ultimate union with, *wish,*
which finds its deepest expression and fulfillment in love.

He begins with a critical explanation of why Freud in his
Victorian culture had to "bring psychoanalysis into being by the
failure of will" (p. 207). He reasons that the Freudian "will of the
Super-ego" is only part of that will in which the individual experiences "his self in its totality," that is, in a "relatively spontaneous
movement in a certain direction" (p. 217). But with a child this
movement begins in opposition, begins in a "no" in denial to his
wish, and from there on it may block love. Like Freud, May sees
this situation as the origin of the *guilt* experience.

Rollo May has made penetrating, analytic studies of the
conflicting as well as interrelating aspects of wish and will in
human life. There are important insights in his comprehensive
delineation of the multitude of aspects of sex and love and in his
discussion of the self and its failures and successes. However, we
must say that ultimately his theorizing represents only a tempting

and innovative version of what is still Freudian theory and not the essentially different approach we need.

Rollo May sees the wish and will conflict as the decisive conflict in human existence. May describes the polarity between pleasure-sex-love-tendencies and the decision for responsible commitment without which the individual cannot move toward self-realization. Unfortunately, however, his customary thoroughness is absent in his rather abrupt "leap to will."

To us it seems that besides the wish and will conflict (if we want to call it so with May) there is another significant conflict to be noted, the strongest manifestations of which are now shaking our Western civilization. It is the conflict between the complacently willing, secure self-adaptation to given circumstances of life and daring creative struggles. Struggles toward what? Toward something which we are not yet able to formulate clearly, something which has to do with new, but as yet indistinct, visions of life, something valuable that will enrich and improve the world. This is the kind of pursuit Hampden-Turner's radical man dares risk, one of personal and universal meaning.

Isn't this what the present youth revolution is all about? Besides enhancing relationships with more love and understanding and equality, young people want to develop study and work conditions that allow for more spontaneity, honesty, depth—in short, creativity—than the present ones do.

Sometimes a person may stifle his creative self-development in favor of *adaptation* to his surroundings. But this adaptation may arouse deep conflicts in his life. Submission to given habitual circumstances may cause guilt feelings as much as does the creative rebellion. This conflict seems to be just as basic as the love-will conflict described by May.

There is, however, an alternative, *positive* form of adaptation—the ever-regenerating *vision* of a fuller, richer reality. Any living being moves into his reality with the expectation and anticipation of being able to extend himself and accomplish some purpose (C. Bühler, 1954). In this arena humans live out the creative struggle that brings new cultural products into being. This is an aspect of human intentionality, in which *cognition* and *conation* are integrated.

To us adaptation is not simply the enforced submission Freud consistently restricts it to being. It is an infant's willingness from the first days of his life to fit in, get along, and belong in the interest of his *security* (which Adler was the first to emphasize as basic).

The ecstasy of creative vision and creative struggle is the only one comparable to the ecstasy of orgasmic love. But its origins are entirely different, because fulfillment through love and fulfillment through creative accomplishment seem to represent two entirely different, though interrelated, motivations and endgoals.

What is human life all about? We hear this question again and again in our psychotherapy sessions. Who can tell? We can only study the lives of people who seem to have found their answers as against those who have not. And invariably the ones who have found the answers are the ones who unswervingly pursued one or both of these ultimate human goals: the give and take of love and dedicated creative accomplishment.

In view of these two different endgoals, the areas of our conflicts are seen as more complicated than conceived of in the wish-will opposition. As Allport (1961) puts it, each of us has many "selves," and integrating them is a tremendous task.

Four basic tendencies in man

In moving toward the two endgoals which promise self-realization and fulfillment, we see four basic tendencies of life (C. Bühler, 1959): (1) the tendency to strive for personal *satisfactions* in sex, love, and ego recognition; (2) the tendency toward self-limiting *adaptation* for the purpose of fitting in, belonging, and gaining security; (3) the tendency toward *self-expression* and creative accomplishments; and (4) the tendency toward integration or *order-upholding*. Conflicts in the individual's self-direction toward his endgoals can be traced all through life to the interplay of these four basic tendencies.

C. Bühler believes that these concepts are necessary for the understanding of the self-directive process as seen by humanistic psychologists. Two processes emphasized by humanistic psychologists can be explained by this schema: (1) the establishment of a personal system of values and goals and (2) the creative process.

The conviction regarding the extraordinary role of *values, goals, and beliefs* in human life is shared, one feels safe in saying, by all humanistic psychologists. Charlotte Bühler (1962) pointed out the problem of weighing responsible value choices against secure adherence to traditional values as a phase of psychotherapy. It has been widely recognized since. She also discussed the relationship of value choices to beliefs. The need for the meaningfulness of our beliefs was emphasized by Frankl (1963) and Maslow (1954).

In the choices required from the individual to establish his values, awareness and thoughtfulness have to be developed. It is widely agreed that our different group processes—be they conducted as continuous therapy groups or as short-term sensitivity training or encounter groups—are helpful in making people aware of how they affect others, how others affect them, and how values and goals may be clarified. These groups are all geared, in different degrees, to completely free and honest self-expression. They initially allow for display of aggression and hostility and attempt to cope with the reality of violent tendencies by acknowledging them as a step toward transformation from the destructive to the constructive.

From earliest childhood values and beliefs are related to order-upholding tendencies which ideally would integrate the expressions of need satisfaction, self-limiting adaptation, and creative expansion. Thus the healthy person will try to integrate the pursuits of pleasure-sex-love needs, his adaptive desire to fit in, and his need to accomplish creatively in the direction of self-realization and fulfillment. He will also strive for a balance between pursuit of his own needs and dedication to self-transcending contributions.

It is rare when a person accomplishes this without frustrations and conflicts, not simply out of self-denial but also as a result of hostilities directed toward him from others. These conflicts may cause him to question the validity of his own efforts.

This sort of doubt shakes our Western civilization today. What sense does it make, some ask, to live with dedication and in the hope of self-realization when we don't even know whether mankind will survive?

A number of young couples don't want to produce children who may have to face hopelessness and destruction in the future. Many people are depressed, not so much by their personal fate as by present events.

Depression and tendencies to suicide were usually considered as expressions of failure to cope with life (Durkheim, 1897). But C. Bühler's research has shown suicidal tendencies to be correlated with failure to accomplish adequate self-realization. That is, tendencies to self-destruction are not necessarily failures of appropriate living but to some extent reactions to seemingly hopeless environmental conditions.

The primary role assigned to man's *creativity* is perhaps the most central concept of humanistic psychology. In American psychological literature, Abraham Maslow (1954) was the first to state that the most universal characteristic of all the people he studied or observed was their creativity. He sees in it "a fundamental characteristic of common human nature—a potentiality given to all human beings at birth." He continues:

> Most human beings lose this as they become enculturated, but some few individuals seem either to retain this fresh and naive, direct way of looking at life, or if they have lost it, as most people do, they later recover it.
>
> This creativeness appears in some of our subjects not in the usual forms of writing books, composing music, or producing artistic objects, but rather may be much more humble. It is as if this special type of creativeness, being an expression of healthy personality, is projected out upon the world or touches whatever activity the person is engaged in. In this sense there can be creative shoemakers or carpenters or clerks. Whatever one does can be done with a certain attitude, a certain spirit that arises out of the nature of the character of the person performing the act. One can even see creatively as the child does. (1954, p. 223).

This creativity, which leads the individual to various self-expressions, is very much in opposition to the need for homeostatic discharge that psychoanalysis has emphasized as the only basic tendency. Contrary to the urge in the direction of relaxing satisfactions, the creatively active person finds elation in his creative tension. This healthy integration of tension of the active person was emphasized first by Goldstein (1939). C. Bühler asserted that the healthy person has alternating needs for activities requiring tension and activities allowing for relaxation.

The most modern American research on creativity has discovered the creative person's predilection for problems that have to be resolved and are not avoided or disliked (as psychoanalysis had taught). Here are some brief quotations from B. Eiduson's (1962) study of chemists:

I really have only *two goals,* I think; the first is the achievement of more understanding of the problems I'm involved with and have been interested in for a long time. The *second goal* I suppose is just to do what I can to help create a world where people can lead decent lives. . . . One thing about science is that the search for understanding is far more exciting than I had ever expected it to be when I was young. It has opened up entirely new vistas of thought that I didn't think existed (p. 157). . . . The pure scientist is one who is interested in a problem because it is interesting and not because it is necessarily going to get him somewhere (p. 158). . . . Their happiness obviously cannot be defined in terms of absence of tension or unabated pleasure. On the contrary, they are very tense about their work, and are frequently impatient and filled with despair; but their discomforts do not dim their over-all notion that what they are doing is enjoyable, and that no other work can compete with it in this respect (p. 161).

The study of creativity has played an outstanding role in European psychology, although it was not seen in terms of motivational and emotional *dynamics,* as humanistic psychology represents it. But if we take as an example Karl Bühler's (1927) demonstrations of creativity in thinking and of creative thinking in play and productivity, we can see the prototype of the dynamic motivational factor.

Creativity as a central concept of humanistic psychology has still another significance. More than any other behavior, it is a manifestation and evidence of the now generally accepted theory that the living being (and especially the human brain) represents an open system with certain freedoms of operation and potentials for change. Again, we believe that Von Bertalanffy applies the open-systems model of the engineer most specifically to the human organism. Of particular interest to the psychologist is his 1968 Clark University lecture "Organismic Psychology and Systems Theory."

Walter Buckley (1967) takes pains to adapt the mechanistic to the organismic point of view:

What is being found appears more and more clearly to be analysable as a highly flexible and efficient information processing servosystem. The gap between stimulus and response is opening wide to make room for the multi-stage mediating processes that alone can account for the differences in behavior between interacting billiard balls and interacting adaptive systems (p. 55).

This expresses what might be considered the central theoretical issue of humanistic psychology: the concept of man as an active mediator of his own existence.

In summary, we have attempted in this chapter to present the thinking of humanistic psychologists and to clarify their concept of a model of man. *Theory* is a necessary goal for the scientist, although it may be unimportant to the nonscientifically involved participant-observer of life. Humanistic psychology has been justifiably criticized when it avoids the theoretical realm. As a scientific endeavor, it must work toward the formulation of a systematic and coherent approach to the psychology of man.

4

Humanistic psychology as related to contemporary culture

As we mentioned in our discussion of the work of K. B. Madsen (1970), a science cannot pretend to be a method of knowing unless its observations are made against the background of the operative *zeitgeist*, or social and cultural climate. So it is that humanistic psychology became one of the prominent forces in psychology at a time when modern man was not only involved with positive striving but also confronted with various negative factors often in serious conflict with positive motivations.

We find a high incidence of *anxiety* and *despair* in young Americans and in their parents. This is true not only of philosophically oriented, introspective young people, who have traditionally been doubtful about the meaning of the universe and their own lives, but also of young people with other orientations. Whereas questioning was the exception among teenagers of the fifties, it seems to be the rule in the seventies.

The sudden immigration of many Europeans to this nation in the postwar years, largely as a result of the earlier Nazi expulsion, served as a stimulus for what we might term a cultural and humanistic renaissance in the United States. This growing respect for and love of the arts and philosophy stimulated a sensitivity toward one's own life and the value of the life of the individual.

What is perhaps even more significant, however, is that the pace of evolution in the United States continued to increase. Although Americans initially were caught up in this rapid development, riding along with it full of the pride of accomplishment and a kind of chauvinistic feeling of invulnerability and hope, the optimistic approach to life was abruptly ended for many in the sixties. Dizzied by the motion of the evolution, they suddenly tried to "stop the world." Many persons realized that, although we had jumped rapidly ahead technologically, we had been hurtled backward in the process in many other vital areas of life. The significance of the individual seemed undermined, and it appeared that life itself was in danger—that our universe could be destroyed with little effort.

With double-edged irony, Stanley Kubrick in *Dr. Strangelove* depicted the destruction of the world within a 24-hour period as a result of one mistake in the programing of a machine. The threat of such overwhelming loss of human life made it impossible for many Americans to maintain their blind faith in the future.

A. Crisis in values—The changing feeling from optimism to pessimism

The beginning of the twentieth century in the United States was typified by optimism as a creed. Visiting Europeans during that era were often surprised and skeptical about how "happy" everyone was all the time. Even at present, when one asks an American how he feels, he will usually tell you with little hesitation that he feels "fine." This response and the hastiness with which it is uttered seem integral, perhaps culturally conditioned. Before the current era it was inappropriate in most circles to admit to *not* feeling good or to answer "lousy," as any Viennese would when not at his best. This has never been standard American etiquette.

In Europe the philosophical thought of more than a century had brought about an expression of pessimism, as was most

clearly demonstrated in the thought of Schopenhauer. This nega-
tivistic approach evinced despair with respect to our human existence (as emphasized by Kierkegaard) and nihilism (as popularized
by Nietzsche). Scientific discoveries have seemed to confound and
challenge the authority of the church in the last two decades in
America, but the statement "God is dead," only now finding its
full reverberations in our country, was made by Nietzsche in 1883.
The problematic nature of human existence was the central subject
of Heidegger's philosophy, and French thinkers like Jean Paul
Sartre and Gabriel Marcel brought these problems closer to people
who were not particularly oriented along philosophical lines.
Writers like Thomas Mann and Herman Hesse (only recently en-
joying popularity in the United States) expressed the mood of
doubt and questioning that was prevalent in Europe as early as
1920.

Today, when you ask young people what they think
would make them happy, it is remarkable (especially in contrast
with the former notion of happiness) that they most frequently
speak of such sober things as contentment, peace, and meaningfulness. Formerly happiness had been engendered by the presence
or promise of external rewards; now it appears that this former
concept is frequently rejected and a deeper notion of the achievement of happiness as a result of internal development is substi-
tuted for it. Many persons, looking about them at real and horrify-
ing dangers and at injustice that has skewed the scales so that some
have much while others have little, consider the idea of happiness
in these times to be blind and frivolous. The concerned thinker of
today often says: "If you tell me you are happy at this moment,
I must tell you that you don't care. You really don't care about
what is happening to *all* of us. You only care that you are having
a good time at this moment."

Scott (1967) questioned 16-year-old high school girls regarding happiness. The three main sources they mention are: (1)
love, (2) scholastic and social success, and (3) inner contentment.
In this last category, besides religious feelings, they speak of satisfaction regarding their own inner growth and development. Perhaps, in the role of students, they felt that sensible answers were
expected of them. But private talks with patients in therapy have
produced similar reactions. For instance, Patty, 16, said in a private
conversation:

> I've had two happy years in my life. The first was at four. I
> remember clearly even now how happy I was. My parents were
> good to me, and, as yet, I didn't have the pressure of school and
> all the obligations to come.
> And this year I am happy for the second time. Why? Because
> I am in love and through this love have gained more understand-
> ing of my boyfriend Bill and of myself.

Personal relationships and the satisfaction that comes
from adequate functioning in them seem to play a decisive role in
the attainment of happiness for these young people. Success seems
secondary in comparison. Another significant factor was "honesty
with one's self." Several of the girls stated that the greatest obstacle to their happiness was "lack of confidence," which often made
them feel "bothersome to other people."

Scott (1967) worked with delinquent girls in an Oregon
state institution and compared their statements with those of the
high school girls. The delinquent girls felt, not surprisingly, that
freedom would be most essential to their happiness. After that
they emphasized good familial relationships as the next most important factor. Several of these girls described their earliest years
as the happiest in their lives. One said "When my parents were
still married, I loved them very much and I felt that the whole
family, even my brother, wanted and loved me" (p. 80). Even in
several popular American magazines the giving of love in relationships is considered a primary condition of happiness. June Callwood (1964) relates the incapacity to give love to confusion and
incoherence in the inner life of a person.

It is interesting to note that in Scott's findings, happiness
does not occur as the result of sensory pleasure alone or from the
currently emphasized "joy"—enchanting and tempting and
momentarily satisfying as this may be. Instead, these young girls
see happiness as derived from loving relationships generated by a
person (or people) whose inner life is integrated and whole, not
disrupted or disturbed. This, of course, is an observation which the
psychotherapist can confirm from his own daily experience with
his clients.

There is much talk about *love* these days, and yet the
concept remains fuzzy and elusive. To the question "What is
love?" no two answers are ever quite the same. Also, we often hear
"I'm not sure that my feeling for this person is love," or "How will
I know when I really love someone?"

"Love" can obviously exist in various guises, even in relation to the same person. Masterful discussions, such as Rollo May's *Love and Will* or Erich Fromm's *Art of Loving*, try to help us toward a deeper understanding of this feeling. Our purpose in the present chapter is not to add yet another elaboration to the discussion; rather, we wish to concentrate on one aspect of love which is particularly within our context.

It is important to stress that, in speaking about love, we do not limit the concept to its specific meaning in the sex-love relationship. Instead, we think of it as an attitude of feeling and caring deeply for another person and as encompassing strong motives to help, to build up, and to enhance this other person's being, separate from one's own being, by giving of oneself. Verbalizations about this form of caring, without correspondent experience, do not ring true.

When we see a play like the recently popular *Hair*, we hear a great deal of elaboration on the word *love*. Actually we believe there are more expressions of hostility than of love in this play. The pregnant girl desperately pursuing and perhaps most needing love is perceived to be essentially alone and uncared for. Eventually she confronts her friends, saying it is "easy to be hard" and "I need a friend."

Encounter groups and modern group therapy have tried to respond to this need for mutual caring. They try to help people who are themselves "lost" or who have never cultivated the ability to be close to another human being. Such closeness, it seems, cannot be replaced by other successes and accomplishments or by the acquisition of material things. And although it cannot alone fill the void in man's existence, this closeness contributes to the meaning of life as a whole.

B. Loneliness

This inability to relate to another person has resulted in what many authors consider a "symptom" customarily found in the troubled man of our times: the widespread feeling of loneliness. In his excellent book on the subject, Clark Moustakas (1961)

distinguishes two principal forms of this emotion. The first he calls
man's *existential loneliness*—the realization of one's aloneness that
seems to be inevitable and reality-oriented, a definition of the
human condition. The second type of loneliness Moustakas discusses is a neurotic reaction consisting of sustained feelings of
self-alienation and self-rejection. Ultimately one must confront
his basic aloneness and assume the responsibility for his own life.
It is significant that, in a time when many are unable to get a grip
on themselves in all the "sound and fury" of modern existence, the
response often is to escape further from the self.

The early Greeks and Romans gave us heroes who were
very much "alone" fighting it out with the elements. Yet the word
lonely, with its connotations of alienation, yearning, and despair,
is not found in translations of these early works. In fact, it seems
to have developed out of the Romantic era, with its concepts of
man's alienation from his society. Allen (1968), pointing out this
semantic development, emphasized that in ancient times the attempt to recover from the bruises of external life was achieved by
turning within for sustenance, as expressed by Marcus Aurelius in
his *Meditations:*

> Men seek retreats for themselves, houses in the country, sea-
> shores, and mountains. . . . But this is altogether a mark of the
> most common sort of men, for it is in thy power whenever thou
> shalt choose to retire into thyself. For nowhere either with more
> quiet or more freedom from trouble does a man retire than into
> his own soul.

In the great period of the Middle Ages, however, man
gave his soul to the Church and his membership always to some
group: the guild, the farm on which he was vassal, the crew which
worked perhaps a lifetime to build Chartres or Mont St. Michel.
Here we see the beginning of man's inability to work things out
for himself and of his dependence on outside sources to save his
soul.

Today's feeling of loneliness occurs in a time when it is
difficult to have faith. The safety of belonging to a group is ne-
gated by the existence of so many groups; often membership in
many does little but fragment the man, and integration of self is
unusual. When man feels lonely now, the emotion is so strong and
all-pervading that it can lead to the feeling of being forsaken, of

being bereaved, of being without help and of not belonging to anyone or anything.

In the Romantic period after Rousseau, the word *lonely* was used most frequently to express the confounding of the natural order by society—the feeling of a person isolated in an insensitive society. For example, in *Werther* Goethe relates loneliness to existence itself; his sorrowful young hero, feeling misunderstood and diminished, says: "Oh, this void! This fearful void which I feel here in my breast!" Unable to find his answer from within, Werther labors under the belief that only union with his unrequited love will bring him the answer, the "cure." But, unable to have his love and unable to find any other meaning in his life, he says: "Yes, it is becoming certain to me, certain and ever more certain, that little importance is attached to the existence of any being, very little."

With the increasing mechanization of our lives, with the doubts of our former faith offered by science, and with the awareness of the immensity of the universe, the agony over our loneliness as human beings has deepened and, in fact, become rooted in our culture. Many of us are not sure that as *individuals* we matter at all. What a strange contradiction there is between the immense importance we assign to ourselves as individuals in our innermost being and, simultaneously, the complete insignificance we seem to have as individuals if viewed from the outside. The world dwarfs us, and many of us feel there is nothing within us substantial enough to make us feel big again.

This concept of loneliness is definitely a product of our present culture with its existential awareness. Feelings of loneliness represent the quintessence of the "human condition," as Hannah Arendt puts it in her brilliant essay of the same name (1958). The search for the meaning of existence begins to haunt the thoughtful adolescent and becomes a stage in his development that formerly was appeased and assuaged by the church and by belongingness in a community of believers. But now this stage may follow the thinking person throughout his life.

These doubts, these feelings of emptiness, cruelly accentuate the loneliness of our time. They throw us back upon need for others, for help through mutual understanding and closeness.

It is interesting that the seeds of this longing for understanding and closeness may already be found in little children. In a simple and basic way, children can feel very lonely. Often we realize this only much later, when we explore childhood memories with an adult patient.

In adolescent development, longing can be viewed as a natural state of mind, the life-style of the child-adult full of the need for love and experiencing the first yearning for a partner of his own. In this period the experience of aloneness is not only natural and normal but perhaps even necessary for later adjustment in the adult world. We call an adolescent "lonely" in our present-day culture in terms of his painful awareness of isolation as an individual and his difficulty in finding closeness and full understanding.

Our modern youth no longer takes for granted that someday everything will be all right or that he will find a real, genuine, and spontaneous closeness, the belonging for which he yearns. He is skeptical about the "American Dream" and its articles of faith, as well as about society's rituals, like courtship and marriage.

Again, the main reason for this doubt lies in the greater awareness of one's own self and of the core of one's own existence. How can a person belong to anything or anyone, how can he be understood, if he does not belong to or understand himself and if he is indeed pulled and torn by his innermost self?

C. Identity

"Who am I?" and "Where am I going?" are two of the most frequently asked questions of our time. It is characteristic of the *zeitgeist* that these questions, expressing so much self-doubt, fear, and uncertainty about goals and direction, are no longer limited to adolescence but may pursue people far into adulthood and, tragically sometimes, into the last period of life, haunting many until death. This problem, no longer resolved simply by emerging from adolescence into adulthood, is really the problem of self—the self that cannot find or name itself and therefore leaves the individual in uncertainty.

A person who is well established within himself feels rather secure in self or perhaps does not even think about the matter of identity at all. In fact, as a grown-up, he is expected to feel sure about these things and to have solved all doubts and indecisiveness about his life. We still maintain the idea that it is "childish" or "adolescent" not to know what one believes in and values, what to expect from the marital partnership, or what to tell one's children when they ask about sex or God or about the chaotic events in social and world affairs.

This chronic uncertainty about beliefs and values and about oneself makes the modern adult feel like a lonely adolescent long beyond the time allotted him to be an adolescent. This phenomenon is now called the *lack of identity* or *loss of identity* and has been specifically labeled as a characteristic of our time and our society.

Actually it is more a lack than a loss, because the concept of loss presupposes that the sense of identity was once there. For many people of our time, identity was never established in the first place. This brings up the question that perhaps identity too must be developed and matured, not simply bestowed as part of the birthright, as a complete and structural part of the organism.

Is this the neurosis of our time? It is a widely discussed question. Allen Wheelis, in his *Quest for Identity* (1958), devotes a careful discussion to this problem, concluding: "Identity is a coherent sense of self. . . . Identity can survive major conflict provided the supporting framework of life is stable, but not when that framework is lost. One cannot exert leverage except from a fixed point."

The uncertainties of modern life may result in the inability of the individual to establish such a core identity, to locate himself in relation to beliefs and values. As a result, he may feel cut off from others, lost and desperate, doubting that anyone can understand him or that he can help himself. "I feel so full of doubt at times," said a 23-year-old patient, "that I cannot even move."

Wheelis distinguishes this modern syndrome from previous forms of neurosis in which definite symptoms seemed to prevail. Although phobias and compulsions were previously felt to be an eruption of repressed impulses, these symptoms are seen today as inadequate and unconscious substitute solutions for more appropriate answers to problems and conflicts. It is important to stress that the common complaints of people in the so-called norm groups of our culture today are much more vague, diffuse, and chronically operative. They are no more emphatic in times of crisis than in everyday life. The etiology of their dilemmas cannot be easily traced to early childhood trauma. Rather, they seem to experience distress because they no longer know who they are or what to live for, and, out of all this, they feel fragmented, lonely, in despair.

An unmarried woman in her late thirties said: "I am conscience-stricken, not because I live sort of a promiscuous life and have various affairs, not because of that really. But I feel guilty because in all of this I'm not developing myself as a person, I'm not really accomplishing anything at all."

This woman's disturbed conscience is not that which Freud referred to as the superego and which represents society's moral code. She is disturbed by what we would nowadays call her *humanistic conscience,* the knowledge that she is not developing her innermost self in bringing out her best potentials to self-realization. Having a grip on one's self, having a knowledge of one's own core motives, allows direction and sureness and what Erikson in his study *Identity: Youth and Crisis* (1968) terms "a subjective sense of sameness and continuity." This means that, regardless of the ebb and flow of the individual within himself and in his interaction with his busy environment, he feels some solid center which allows him to push out his "force" and to expand himself, rather than to escape and feel diminished.

The particular kind of lonely despair that these troubled people feel results partially from the fact that they do not just naïvely call themselves "sick." They are aware of the reality of their struggle to find a central core in themselves, to find suitable goals and so to lead a meaningful existence.

A poem by a boy student expresses this well:

> Why can't we know where we are going?
> Why can't we be sure
> Where the road will lead?
> Traveling blind.
>
> Why, if I know my goal so clearly
> Is the road so dark?
> Is it just a shadow
> Hiding the light?
>
> How can I run if the sea
> Has made me an island?
> Far from the shore,
> Never knowing who I am.

I'll never stop 'til I can stand there
Where a man's a man.
We will stand together,
When we arrive.

R. Craig Bühler

"Why can't we know where we are going? Why can't we be sure where the way will lead?" This is one of the most general yet overwhelming problems of our time, not only for young people but for practically everyone.

Some youths discuss these questions with their elders. In contrast to the rigidly conservative and the rebellious groups, these constructive young people, acknowledging the necessity for improvement in our personal and social lives, try to work out new solutions with the help of trusted older people. They need help in finding deeper, more valid beliefs and values; they want assistance in freeing their creativity to bring out their best potentials.

What makes it so difficult for the older generation, who presumably are the leaders or, better, the guides, is that we cannot tell them anything positively. The task of the last generation's parents was especially difficult. They were unsure of their own positions, their views, their techniques, and their roles in their children's lives. Psychoanalysis had made them completely insecure concerning their influence. Perhaps Dr. Spock's tremendous success derived to a great extent from the fact that he told parents not to worry too much.

Now, however, not only parents but every thinking person must reevaluate his concept of existence as a human and his orientation in directing himself and others who ask his help and advice. It is at this point that humanistic psychology can be of help, since it has made great strides in dealing with these problems.

As was previously mentioned, a fundamental tenet of humanistic psychology is the pursuit of values, which are seen as inherently needed by humans. This pursuit receives its directives from the self, which is considered a central core system, continuously present in nuclear form from the beginnings of the individual's life. In this theory there is a decisive divergence with psychoanalysis, which regarded the pursuit of values as a secondary goal —a goal pursued under the pressure of society when the individual's drives could not otherwise be satisfied.

Humanistic psychologists assume that the pursuit of certain values furthers the development of one's own potentialities and the fulfillment of one's own innermost needs. In the discovery of his unique potentialities, an individual may need assistance. And here is where the humanistic psychotherapist comes into the picture—in helping the individual toward the establishment of his own identity.

After the individual has found a direction for his self, he can pursue a second important goal: involvement in meaningful relationships. Carl Rogers (1961) discusses this development in detail.

Many young people, and some older people as well, are dedicated to finding new methods for enabling people to better understand and tolerate each other. As one young coed commented, "Our attitudes are more an emphasis on relationships."

This feeling is movingly expressed by the laborer Yefrim Poduyev in Solzhenitsyn's novel *The Cancer Ward* (1969). Poduyev, a simple man who has labored hard and whored hard during his whole life, has never been ill for a single day but now finds himself sick and doomed in the stultifying cancer ward. He has become confused about life and everything in it. Poduyev has never read a book. But now he has nothing else to do, and by chance he picks up a little volume and focuses on an article headed by the question "What do people live by?" This question becomes *his* question, and he moves about the cancer ward asking it of everyone. He receives various answers. "By rations, by wages, by their trade," the people say. He himself had believed so previously. But the little volume tells him this is a delusion. "People live by love," says Leo Tolstoy.

And this seems to be a commonality among all of us. It was felt by one of the authors of this book while working with an institutionalized child.

To Gail, Whom They Call Schizophrenic

I race after you,
playing
that I am a "giant monster,"
and I wonder
whose voice you hear
and what the nature
of the fear.
I sit beside you

as you draw again
the tiny boat
in endless waves
and I wonder
if it is something
you have seen
in some far-away reality
or in dreams
I will never experience
no matter how close you allow.
Little things—
your hand on the turtle's shell,
stroking,
the day you first talked,
pointing at a picture
on the wall,
telling me
"That is mine,"
your eyes, unfocused,
and that rare sharpness
when they sought something,
the candy you kept stealing
even after being punished.
I hold you against me,
your head inside my jacket,
your body shaking,
thin sapling in a foreign wind,
and I wonder
if you feel me touching you
and if you have any knowledge
of your own deep-lost, never-dead
child warmth.
You are isolated
on a playground,
I kneel beside you
and the two of us
are isolated.
Man, however "healthy,"
is isolated,
adrift in the Universe.
That, in *my* words,
is the essence of All you know.
Will it be possible
for you to accept,
deal,
transcend?
Will you ever know
you are worthy of Love?

Melanie Allen

D. Authority

Another issue that seems to fit significantly into the present pattern in our culture is the problem of *authority*. Out of a strong allegiance to the Judeo-Christian ethic, authority was once easily accepted. But today authority per se represents a dubious value. Leadership is no longer automatically possessed of the magic power and right to control or even influence and guide people.

The *generation gap*, which as Feuer claims in his brilliant chronology (1969), has always existed, has become in itself a cause for open fighting and rebellion. An example of this conflict is found in *The Gap* (1968), by Lorber and Fladell. Ernie and his nephew Richie attempt to find ways of understanding each other. Uncle Ernie even goes as far as to travel into the strongholds of New York hippiedom with Richie, and Richie works for a short time in Ernie's business. In the end Richie feels that his uncle has learned very little from what he has seen. Richie writes: "I began to think of him as a martyr of enlightenment, but really more interested in being martyred than enlightened." Richie himself remains unconvinced that "making a living" is "worthwhile enough as a goal of life." We must agree with him fully.

If the older generation's best advice to the younger is centered around the virtues and values of "making a living," it is easy to see why young people are saying "to hell with you." "Making a living"—what a miserable definition of a primary goal; it is not even "making a life." Perhaps those adults who express their goals in this way are not doing themselves justice, for surely those who devote themselves to making their families happy are already doing a good deal more than just "making a living."

Such pat phrases reveal something, however. They demonstrate that the older generation either has forgotten or perhaps never learned to think about the values and objectives of an adequate human existence. So the younger generation is justifiably dubious about the right of the Establishment to wield power over others, since, if these persons have no respect for life itself or for their own lives, how can they be trusted with influence over others?

The conflict with authority figures usually stems from

relationships within the family. The parents of today's adolescents have been extremely lenient with their children, partly because of the impact of psychoanalysis and partly in opposition to the rigidly authoritarian generation that preceded them. Frequently, however, their permissiveness conflicted with the value structure under which *they* had been raised, and many swung back at times toward the more rigid structure. These insecurities and inconsistencies resulted in what the children interpreted as weakness or hypocrisy, which often led them to contempt and, in extreme cases, hatred.

Other parents were so preoccupied with their own problems that they devoted little time to their children or, if they did, often foisted their emotional confusion on them. Although these parents might have maintained some vague ideals about their children's development, their behavior, and particularly the punishment they meted out, was frequently a displacement of personal frustration rather than a consistent adherence to any set of principles.

There were, of course, parents of this last generation who used no discipline at all and offered no guidance in the lives of their children. At the same time some people managed to maintain a solid system of values, but, sadly—and there are few statistics to validate this hypothesis—it seems that this group was in the minority.

Albert Szent-Györgyi, the great Hungarian scientist and humanist famous for his discovery of vitamin C, writes in *The Crazy Ape* (1970), a critique of our society and culture, that we have a gerontocracy operative in this nation, an old system with old values. He says it is "a good system when changes are slow and the main problem is the preservation of values, but gerontocracy becomes highly dangerous in periods of rapid change, such as the present period . . . when man's existence depends on his ability to adjust to and create a new world."

In an early study C. Bühler (1941) compared the attitudes toward authority of European youngsters with a long tradition of strict discipline behind them with those of American youths whose families represented islands of disciplinarian upbringing in the midst of predominantly lenient communities. The children of these "isolated authoritarians" frequently exhibited chronic guilt and neurotic hatred of authority. Their resentment stemmed from their inability to cope with experienced injustice, hypocrisy, lack of understanding, and, sometimes, lack of love.

Psychoanalysis had made people aware of all the hostility they harbored in the unconscious—hostility they had carried around inside them for perhaps many years. This poisoning emotion had its origin in the individual's relationship with his parents and was then transferred to other persons and, beyond them, to the institutions that seemed to protect and even enhance authority as principle. Psychoanalysis tried to teach people to express these feelings outwardly and thus to learn to free themselves from the burden of this hate.

Here, however, another facet came to the fore, because, as indicated earlier, this hatred of authority was not solely a neurotic reaction to personally experienced hardships. Much of it actually became an objective doubt about the principle of authority as such. People came to question the wisdom claimed not only by older, more experienced persons, but also by institutions set up and presupposed to have authority by virtue of their continued functioning (such as administrative, educational, and religious bodies). Although serviceable for various functions and recognized and used by many for these functions, the values these institutions proclaimed they stood for often seemed not really valid or essential or even often adhered to.

The older generation and their predecessors, those who had on good faith built up what we now call the Establishment, were sharply criticized by the younger generation for being hypocritical in professing virtues which they did not really have. They also were accused of having formed a power structure through which they protected themselves and which offered the individual who belonged to it not only a fortress but also a hiding place.

In their resistance to the authority and hypocrisy of their elders, the attackers focused on a number of serious issues. We shall now discuss some of these problems.

E. Meaningfulness

Viktor Frankl (1963) can be given credit for reawakening interest in the concept of life's meaningfulness. Although this concept had a long history, until recently modern psychology had little consideration for it, largely because it seemed scientifically inaccessible.

It is true that a strict scientific model simply does not seem to be able to cope with the more complex, waxing, and waning inner experiences of man. Frankl admits to this and rejoices in the fact that there is yet something of man which cannot be explained.

In biographical studies by C. Bühler (1933), *meaning* was clearly demonstrated to be a significant factor in many life histories, for people would say in looking back over their lives that they either had been meaningful or had lacked meaning. What are they referring to in using this term?

Meaningfulness, as we speak of it (although admittedly our definition may be ill-fated), refers to a special kind of content of life experience which makes life seem richer, fuller, more worthwhile. Life without meaning feels worthless and empty. Frankl speaks of this feeling as the existential vacuum. Meaningfulness, then, seems to be an essential factor in human existence. But how is it experienced? What are its characteristics?

In the biographical studies just referred to and in recent case studies, C. Bühler found that people call their lives meaningful when they live for something they believe in. This something may be a particular goal, a cause, or perhaps another person to whom they are dedicated. What this seems to indicate is that, although the sense of direction and motivation and impetus comes from within the healthy person, the goal of the force is outside of or beyond one's self.

Frankl (1963) calls this experience *self-transcendence*. In using this term, he indicates his belief that, in this highest of all life-states, we feel a deep necessity to relate to and dedicate ourselves to something outside ourselves. Maslow (1961) has taken up this concept, and both he and Frankl think of self-transcendence as the ultimate self-fulfillment. We, too, consider this concept highly valid.

"What do you live for?" one of us once asked in a group, when one of the members was complaining about lack of direction.

"What do you mean, what do I live for?" was the somewhat hostile retort of Rod. "I just live."

"I live to get ahead, to be rich one day, I suppose, and to be important," said Dick.

"But," Don questioned him, "would this *really* satisfy you

in the long run? Isn't the fact that you are here really saying that you're dissatisfied with yourself?"

Some of the younger groups often debate whether anything makes sense at all in this life, when so many things are wrong with their world and when any day they might be drafted and sent off to fight and perhaps die in a war they cannot believe in. They look around and see some of the simple beauties of the world ruined. In short, they see mankind as self-destructive.

"I know I won't go and let myself be killed," says Keith, who is 22. "So if they *do* call me up, I'm getting out of the country. I don't believe in any killing at all. But, even though I know I don't believe in *that,* I really don't know what I *do* believe in. What can I do that makes sense?"

There are several obstacles to discovering what is meaningful in one's own life. Many people are not ready for consideration of such questions as meaningfulness because they are still totally preoccupied with emotional conflicts and unsatisfied needs. *Gladys,* for example, reports that she doesn't know what people mean when they speak of "meaningful living." She would be content if she could find anything in her life that satisfied her, but she feels torn in many directions, none of which seem to relate to each other.

Another problem is engendered when people must face the fact that they really don't know what they are best suited for or what they should do with their lives. Humanistic psychology deals with this dilemma as being very different from former psychiatric syndromes, referring to it as the problem of discovering and bringing out *one's best potentials.*

People with special talents seem to suffer much less frequently from this problem, unless emotional conflicts hinder their development. Steve, for instance, is highly gifted scientifically; he went to college with the intention of pursuing a career in science, feeling that he could be truly *useful* as a scientist and therefore would have a meaningful future. At about the same time he fell in love with a girl who returned his feelings, although he had previously experienced difficulty in love relationships. The humanistic psychologist would feel that Steve had now developed the capacity to bring out his best potentials both in his work and in his interpersonal relationships. This maturation and the chance to give and take in *both* these endeavors gave him the experience of meaningfulness.

A third problem interfering with the establishment of a meaningful existence is one which we have repeatedly alluded to in this chapter. It is the difficulty encountered by people in finding objectives and values they can believe in, given the modern world. If things cease to make sense, they certainly fail to be convincing objectives.

Marvin, for example, had planned to study engineering. But he deeply condemned modern industry for its abuse of man-power. He seriously doubted that Western civilization was continuing to move in the direction of progress. He quit school and joined the hippie movement in its early stages. His particular group lived withdrawn from society proper in tents and supported themselves by making and selling primitive earthenware. Soon, however, this way of life did not seem to hold the answer *for him* any longer. He eventually came into psychotherapy to work out the problem of values—to find what *he,* Marvin, could believe in and live for.

Many young people are entering therapy in just this way, in what we call an *existential crisis,* which—we again stress—does not revolve around an isolated happening in life. The following passages consist of excerpts from the writings and journals of some of these patients during the time of their therapy, when they were trying to find themselves through something they had created.

Here, for instance, is a poem by a young girl, formerly a student but now in a kind of limbo land:

> I'm going to Berkeley
>   to find some friends
>   something to believe in
>   for a while at least again
> To do my own thing
>   dress the way I want
>   feel a part of the Revolution
>   (whether there is one or not)
>   so many things to believe in
>   so many ways to turn
> Ah—but I am apart at the seams
>   and so is this scene
> Split into splinters
>   of triumphant "make-belief"
> So you leave one scene
>   exchange it for another
>   in another country or another city

> But it always comes down to the same old thing
>   the System is rotten—but so am I
> And finally—at the end of it all
> You come round to see
> That systems aren't where it's at
> And you say—O.K.—or—oh no—shit
> And fuck the whole thing
>   and go lie on the beach—
> But if you care at all
>   and you do because you're still here
> Then you laugh in meaningless patches
> Light fires without matches
>   cover your body with ashes
>   and take a trip—to there—and back to here—nowhere
> And you never face the scandal
>   that there's nothing you can handle
>   because everything—moving at the speed of light
>   is so huge—so far away
> And you can't go home again
>   and you can't really stay here
> And somewhere in you—you really believe
>   there must be a meaning—somewhere.

Margaret Levers

The following excerpt from the journal of a young writer currently in therapy records his memory of a life dialogue concerning identity and meaning:

"Do you *really* know who you are?" says the spunky little blonde, a few of her hangups showing.

HE: "I know who I am."

SHE: "Well, that's really great."

ME to ME: Yes, great, if I am to believe you. And why am I seeming to be prepared to *not* believe you? I don't know who I am. I know a lot about what I think I'm not. I know a lot about the many compartments—focal planes—that are me. But I must relocate that point in time and environment when the self did not congeal. . . .

Now D. says: "A person has to set goals for himself . . . all kinds . . . from the 'short-term material' to the 'long-term this-is-where-I-want-to-be.' And every year he has to ask himself . . . Am I *on time?*"

HE: "You make life sound like an installment plan."

Nobody's listening to me, but I speak to the smoky air anyway: He's right, you know . . . that "on time" thing is really important—necessary—intrinsic—vital. . . .

SHE says to D.: "Are you where you want to be?"

D.: "Of course not. And if I ever get there, I might as well be dead. I *was* almost there . . . but I had to start all over again . . . approach it in different ways. You see, I had this big field of corn . . . but someone came in the night and chopped it all down." (His young lover had recently died an untimely death, at 26.)

The writer continues to muse: This is a non-story from the nowhere land overlooking the canyon of insanity—longing to fall over the precipice into mindless oblivion—but knowing it is not permitted. Simply, not permitted. No visible reasons, answers, explanation. For they are on the other side of "you-can-do" mountains in know-thyself land. Nowhere land—where the walls are made of mirrors and the streets are paved with excrement—where beds are of hands—sand is water and water is sand.

Which one of the seven dwarfs am I?
or am I really prince charming in snow white drag?
the witch I am not, though a witch I become
"Nowhere man . . . singing all his nowhere songs for
   nobody."

McLaughlin Smith

And these are not the characteristically alienated and rebellious youth but confused and unhappy youths looking for a new type of guidance. Often, when guidance is not to be had, the lack of connection with one's life goes as far as to result in the former kind of traumatic crisis. An extremely famous couple in literature, the F. Scott Fitzgeralds, gradually fell away from contentment with their early fame and success, into a long and empty period of loneliness and despair. For Zelda, the end was institutionalization, and this tragic happening resulted in increasing apathy, alcoholism, and defeat for Scott. In an article written while in the Southern institution where she later ended her life, Zelda (1934) stated (remembering what was now past forever):

> We walked at night towards a cafe blooming with Japanese lanterns, white shoes gleaming like radium in the damp darkness. It was like the good gone times when we still believed in summer hotels and the philosophies of popular songs. Another night we danced a Wiener Waltz and just simply swept around together.

And Scott, alone, trying to get himself together in a Southern hotel room, wrote what was later to be the beginning of *The Crack-Up* (1931):

I had a strong sudden instinct that I must be alone. I didn't want to see people at all. I had seen so many people all my life —I was always saving or being saved—it was not an unhappy time. I went away and there were fewer people. I found that I was good-and-tired. I could lie around and was glad to, sleeping or dozing sometimes twenty hours a day and in the intervals trying resolutely not to think—instead I made lists—made lists and tore them up, hundreds of lists . . . and then suddenly, surprisingly, I got better . . . and (then) cracked like an old plate. . . . I realized that in those years, in order to preserve something —an inner hush maybe, maybe not—I had weaned myself from all things I used to love—and things, but only followed the rickety old pretense of liking. I saw that even my love for those closest to me was become only an attempt to love, that my casual relations . . . were only what I remembered I *should* do, from other days . . . all rather inhuman and undernourished, isn't it? Well, that, children, is the true sign of cracking-up. . . . I am a slowthinking man, and it occurred to me simultaneously that of all natural forces, vitality is the incommunicable one. . . .

YE ARE THE SALT OF THE EARTH, BUT IF THE SALT HATH LOST ITS SAVOUR, WHEREWITH SHALL IT BE SALTED?*

The Fitzgeralds, representative of a *first* "lost" generation, writing at the time of World War II—at a time when the romance and dreams of their life were lost and nothing within or without seemed to give them reason to go ahead—show in their loneliness and apathy and fatigued defeat much the same kind of syndrome that our disillusioned young people and adults illustrate today. And it is this kind of problem that concerns the humanistically oriented psychologist: the chronic dilemma of life in a lonely and uncertain time and of finding *one's own source of vitality and purpose* within such a time.

*F. Scott Fitzgerald, *The Crack-Up*. Copyright 1934, 1936 by Esquire, Inc., 1945 by New Directions Publishing Corporation. Reprinted by permission of New Directions Publishing Corporation, New York, and The Bodley Head Limited, London.

5

The importance of humanistic psychology in the contemporary perspective: Applications and innovations in psychotherapy and education

A recurrent thread in the fabric of this little book has been our feeling that the twentieth-century scientist can no longer feel safe in the sanctity of his laboratory. Neither, for that matter, is the classical setting of the clinician's chamber as isolated sanctuary an appropriate image to present reality. Both researcher and clinician, if they are dedicated to studying and serving mankind, are confronted daily with the complicated and pressing cultural crisis in Western civilization. To turn one's back on the course of evolution, pretending that one can capture all the relevant variables in one's own laboratory, one's own office, or the cloistered classroom, is deceptive and unjust to those one serves. Essential to the stance of the modern scientist is the fact that, despite his profession, he too is a human being. His investment is a personal one, in that the fruits of his work may help to sustain his *own* life.

The spreading influence of humanistic psychology in the decade of the sixties stemmed partially from its awareness of these facts. The humanistic psychologist in his willingness to risk the role of scientific revolutionary paralleled the acts of revolutionaries against other institutions whose rigidly authoritarian positions threatened the course of modern life. The humanistic psychologist allied himself with the youth of our country in their desperate urge to regain what had been lost in the human experience. Often he served as a friend and adviser to innovators who moved into the community in an attempt to turn such institutions as the mental health clinic, the university, the public school, and the prison inside out in order that old, dated structures could be re-evaluated and replaced with better ones. His own image of man, that metaphilosophical vision we delineated earlier in this work, recognized that organism and environment interact and fluctuate together and that forces externally operative can so impinge on the individual as to corrode and corrupt that which is most essentially human.

In a sense, this humanistic and relativistic credo has come to replace the more structured and fading absolutist tradition of the church. As Sidney Jourard (1964) put it, the humanistic psychologist recognizes and reacts to and with the "spirit" of man. We agree with Jourard's discussion of evincing man's need to fulfill himself and to find meaning in life. Again, humanistic psychology has become an important force as its metaphilosophical position of belief in man's ability to exercise his own potential toward the creation of a positive life has in many ways replaced the need for externally operative religious systems. *Man is learning to have faith in himself.*

A. Humanistic psychology and its applications in contemporary psychotherapy

The humanistic psychologist does not turn away from confrontation with the absurd world of today. He cannot afford to. He does not separate his clients or himself from these concerns. He sees his own activities—personally, professionally, therapeutically—as issuing naturally out of these factors.

This credo is an approach to life as a whole. It is a recognition that the therapist-researcher and the client-subject share more than anything else in the communality of their humanity. By this we mean to indicate the acceptance of human potential and the acceptance of individual limitations. Perhaps the deepest bond in the therapist-client relationship or in the teacher-student relationship emerges out of this unspoken recognition.

James Bugental (1971) speaks of all this as the "humanistic ethic," which he describes as postulating that "each person is the most responsible agency in his own life." Regardless of social pressures and external contingencies, this ethic "insists that the person is not displaced from being the one who mediates all such influences and in large part determines how they will influence his being." He relates this concept to what Rollo May (May, Angel, & Ellenberger, 1958) called "centeredness." Bugental uses "humanistic ethic" interchangeably in most instances with "therapeutic ethic" and with "growth orientation." We feel that this ethic is an essential factor underlying the process of humanistic psychotherapy and a foundation for our discussion of applying humanistic psychology to psychotherapy.

In further defining the factors he feels are inherent to an ethical approach in any humanistic encounter, Bugental establishes a pattern which may be implicit as the motif in this new school's application to psychotherapy. His main tenets are as follows:

1. Although the basic postulation is that the individual is the most responsible agent in his own life, this should not be interpreted as "a counsel of isolation or of unreal self-centeredness. . . . Claiming and accepting subjecthood in one's own life is a necessary pre-step to any valid encounter with another person, and it means accepting responsibility for one's own actions and experience, rather than acting as though licensed for self-indulgence."

2. "The ideal for relationships between people is one of mutuality between persons each of whom is the subject of his own life and each of whom values and recognizes the subjecthood of the other." Bugental indicates that this is Martin Buber's "I-Thou" relationship (1958).

3. The humanistic ethic puts forth an existential or "here-and-now" perspective emphasizing that "one always lives only at

the present moment." This concept of the vitality contained in "the everflowing present . . . is expressed when a person seeks to know as well as possible what it is he is experiencing at each moment and what is the genuine nature of the situation in which he finds himself."

4. The humanistic ethic recognizes that nonhedonistic emotions "such as pain, conflict, grief, anger, and guilt are parts of the human experience to be understood and even valued rather than suppressed and hidden." Bugental stresses that, contrary to simply being a "disorganized response," expression of an emotion symbolizes "an experienced meaning in the person's life."

5. People who have truly incorporated the humanistic ethic are united in seeking "growth-facilitating experiences."

Bugental goes on to describe the "collision" of the humanistic ethic with the condition of contemporary society. Integral to his scheme is his emphasis that the humanistic therapist-educator-person hopes that via his interventions and interactions he himself and the individual with whom he is interacting will *"emerge from that experience as societal change agents themselves"* (italics ours). The humanistic dialogue and the humanistic credo can therefore actively function toward the reformation of those structural elements in contemporary society which are detrimental and corrupting to the maintenance and sustenance of rich and vital living. We feel that this point is most crucial to our discussion in this book and to our continued avowal that the humanistic scientist and therapist is himself actively aware of the context of his own existence and of his ability to influence that existence, internally and externally. By the same token, his feeling of commonality with those to whom he relates means that he anticipates that they also possess this active and positive power.

In summary, Bugental's delineation contains within it all those factors that we ourselves feel are characteristic of humanistic psychology as it applies to the therapeutic experience (and, in fact, to any relationship or intervention).

We must credit Carl Rogers (1942, 1951) with first introducing a new, humanistic concept of the therapist-patient relationship. He also suggested new procedures in and attitudes toward psychotherapy which differed distinctly from the previously prevailing psychoanalytic techniques, as well as from more recently developed principles and methods of behavior therapy.

Rogers has had a great impact in the area of psychotherapy, and many psychologists have identified in most respects with his approach to therapy as well as with his concepts of personality development and personality change.

We believe that a singular merit of historical consequence in Rogers' work is the fact that he has made psychotherapeutic procedures accessible to study in records and on tape. Until this innovation, therapy had been treated either as an occult science or as a sanctified mystery or rite. Rogers was courageous in challenging this notion of the ingroup secret and opening up the possibility for analysts and nonanalysts to examine and compare the happenings in the psychotherapeutic process. Students could observe and research the comparative effects of different techniques, therapists, and personalities on individual patients.

Rogers not only hypothesized but practiced a completely new pattern of procedures in treating clients. We will now discuss the most outstanding and widely accepted characteristics of what he termed the *client-centered approach.*

From the point of view of the psychoanalyst, the therapist-patient relationship could not be characterized as other than one of *transference.* That is, the relationship must develop as a repetition of the patient's emotional relationships in childhood with one (or both) of his parents. From this source will ensue the ultimate "cure," for, through reliving the old, unresolved conflicts of the past with the therapist as parent-symbol, a solution and later elimination of these conflicts can naturally proceed.

Admittedly, transference relationships cannot always be avoided, but more important to the humanistic psychotherapist is the establishment of a person-to-person relationship. Rogers finds that this mutual interaction is more instrumental in the development of trust and acceptance than is the highly emotional relationship of dependency characteristic of the transferring patient in the Freudian setting. One factor in Bugental's humanistic ethic is the development of mutuality in relationships.

Various humanistic psychotherapists have developed variations on this person-to-person relationship. Rogers himself has recommended a role which he first called nondirective but later modified to a more active participation. Even with this change of attitude, however, he still speaks of the therapist as a "facilitator," an expression which many of the more involved therapists might reject. Eugene Gendlin (1967), one of Rogers' students, differs from his mentor's system in strongly emphasizing the sharing of feelings between himself and his patients. Arthur Burton (1967) thinks that the therapist represents, in the Jungian sense, "the other" in the patient's life and that "being-with" is a basic human need. We should mention in this regard that Jung and other neoanalysts such as Adler, Rank, and Ferenczi were all precursors to the Rogerian concept of the humanistic therapist-to-patient relationship. Burton's emphasis of the direct and more immediate participation of the therapist in his client's life is again characteristic of the I-Thou encounter Martin Buber envisioned.

The humanistic psychologist considers the discovery of adequate values and beliefs as one of the most complex and pressing problems of our time. C. Bühler (1962) pointed out that assisting the patient in the clarification of his personal value system is one of the modern therapist's main tasks. Jourard (1968, 1969) went as far as to recommend a "guru-like" role of the therapist as guide, much in the sense of the Eastern mentor-leader. His emphasis on the "spiritual" quality of the human relationship directed him to this notion, although he himself has gradually modified it to a belief in a more equal and shared relationship. He theorizes and presents considerable research (1964) on the importance of self-disclosure on the part of the therapist as well as the client, so as to create the depth of experience obtained when two people search for meaning together. We shall elaborate upon Jourard's work at a later point in this chapter.

Rogers stressed a second point that we believe to be of major significance in humanistic therapy: the importance and impact of the personality of the therapist in the process of counseling. The psychoanalyst feels protected by his presence as an authority figure. But the humanistic therapist recognizes and utilizes his own frailty, his own experience. He shares the human dilemma and can risk stepping out of a more elevated, deified role to admit to this. In psychoanalysis techniques were a major factor, whereas the success of humanistic psychotherapy depends to a great extent on the therapist's discovery of individually tailored methods of communicating with his patient to impress upon him those things which they share. Bugental (1965) emphasized his own adequacy as a person and his authenticity in the give-and-take of the therapeutic relationship. In several studies reviewed by Truax and

Carkhuff (1964), success in psychotherapy was highly correlated with the genuineness, competence, self-confidence, and expressiveness of the psychotherapist as a person. We shall discuss therapeutic research in more detail later.

A third point emphasized by Rogers is humanistic psychotherapy's general orientation to the growth, development, and education of the human being as a person. This orientation issues out of Maslow's emphasis on growth-motivation rather than deficiency-motivation.

The humanistic psychologist, like the behaviorist, does not focus his attention on *labeling* and *diagnosis*. Instead, he emphasizes emotional problems, stress, indecision, and conflict regarding value choices as part and parcel of the universal condition in this increasingly difficult and demanding era of shakeup, disruption, and accelerated evolution.

Allen Wheelis (1958), who was originally a psychoanalytically oriented psychiatrist, now points out that we no longer deal with "neurotics" in the old sense but with people who have lost or never found direction, who have no values in which they can believe, and who are, as Rollo May (1953) put it, in search of themselves. As mentioned previously, this identity problem was first brought to the fore by Erik Erikson (1950), but his discussion was confined to its importance in the development and maturation of the adolescent. In our own discussion on identity, we indicated that a singularly modern aspect has been the occurrence of identity crises in adult lives.

The humanistic psychologist expands upon the words of the Delphic Oracle, *"Know thyself,"* urging *"Be* thyself." Charlotte Bühler (1962) wrote of a young woman who for years had been enmeshed in a conflict of divided loyalties to her mother and to her husband. The mother lived with the couple in their apartment and was chronically hysterical, demanding, and draining of her daughter's energies. The background of the family was German, and traditional German morality was insistent on "honoring one's parents" above all. The husband tried for a long time to be a dutiful son-in-law and repress his own antagonisms, although he felt the mother to be quite capable of living alone if certain domestic help were provided. The wife continued to be so pressed by her mother that more and more she neglected her relationship with her husband, although she loved him very much. Ultimately, the husband could no longer contain his feelings and frankly insisted that, with their help, the mother move to her own apartment. He felt that, if the wife did not agree to the new arrangement, their marriage was doomed. Faced with succumbing to the demands of her mother or obeying her husband's wishes (which were her own inclinations), she was able eventually to accept her husband's solution as that which she herself believed in and to act on this awareness. In using this example, Bühler emphasized her belief in the importance of personal honesty and illustrated the tragic situations often engendered by obedience to abstract "codes" that cause sacrifice of self.

This need to understand one's self and to build an adequate self that can form satisfying and mutual relationships was felt by Rogers to be so universal and currently relevant that he recommended this psychotherapy process as beneficial and educational even for so-called normal persons.

Both individual and group psychotherapy accentuate an opening up of feelings as they are experienced, in line with that tenet of the humanistic ethic emphasizing the "ever-flowing moment" (Bugental, 1971) or the "here-and-now." The concept behind the idea of *encounter* issues partially from the notion that participation in the process of building relationships leads to an integration within the individual of knowledge about how a personality forms, functions, and can change and grow. To experience directly and intensely what it means to be a person in this world would establish a deep base for understanding the self and others.

Although this new approach was first applied in training groups, encounter groups, and sensitivity groups, many humanistic psychologists felt that, through these interactions, foundations would carry over into the society and form the basis for a new kind of constructive and meaningful interrelationships between people. Thomas Greening (1971) reinforces our position that this sort of experience can lead members to a state of being that approaches the religious experience.

In a wave of enthusiasm and hope, group meetings quickly spread. The concept of encounter for developing awareness and sensitivity in personal interactions was introduced and incorporated in many institutions. Educators and business administrators were eager to utilize this new process to provide more satisfying environments and experiences for their members. Bradford, Gibb, and Benne (1964) were particularly important in applying their expertise in this area to business and industry. Fred Massarik was influential in spreading these new procedures to many other countries. His international approach led in 1970 to his founding (with C. Bühler) of the *International Journal of Interpersonal Development*. The impetus behind this journal was the belief that these new methods were means by which individuals could communicate across physical and national boundaries to sponsor personal and social changes addressed to the cultural crisis in Western civilization and the universality of mankind.

With this sudden and tumultuous development, facets of the group movement emerged that became highly controversial. Humanistic therapists themselves differed regarding their goals for what was soon seen to be a powerful new technique. The here-and-now experience became a slogan for many of the participants in the group movement and led to an emphasis—and later to an absolute concentration—on the encounters themselves. Although Rogers himself favored the existential approach (as did other humanistic psychologists like Greening, Jourard, and May), he did not anticipate the degree to which this approach would be overinterpreted to sanction all manner of fads. Rogers (1967) responded with a systematic presentation of the values and hazards of encounter groups. He delineated a series of stages in the group process, from original negativeness and resistance to a fullness of expression and exploration of personally meaningful material. His positive stress was on the healing capacity of the group, the *beginnings* of change, and the open expression of emotion. Although he admitted to the dangers and disadvantages in the group experience, he expressed the need for concentration on the *goal* behind this movement. According to Rogers, the group process helps members to become "more spontaneous, flexible, closely related to their feelings, open to their experiences, and closer and more expressively intimate in their interpersonal relationships." These goals are certainly representative of qualities that would be supported by the humanistic ethic.

Many humanists themselves have assumed critical positions regarding certain aspects of encounter. One common complaint is that the effects are not long-lasting or penetrating enough to bring about self-knowledge, new behaviors, and the discovery of new directions. Also, many groups operating today are led by untrained and unlicensed individuals who go far beyond meaningful experience. These groups, pointing to what has been called heightened awareness and transpersonal experience, concentrate on the unpredictable, the ecstatic, and the mystical.

Greening (1971) is convinced of the benefits inherent in what may emerge as "religiosity" in the group experience, but he is wary of the "Pandora's box" that has been opened in the instantaneous development of this movement. Allen (1970a) alluded to the dangers inherent in the group process and the possible tragedies engendered by misuse of the new techniques. She also emphasized the importance of carryover into the real lives of the members:

> Among the skills we have perfected in this country is the refined facility for game-playing. Although responsible sensitivity trainers are critical of untrained leadership in encounter groups, nevertheless the encounter movement often carries with it the essence of Fun and Games; numerous branches of the movement, perhaps without wanting to, have left the concept of Basic Encounter. This has happened because their opener or catalyst has become for fearful participants the focus and, instead of being an "easy way in," the gimmick serves also as an "easy way out." We see then a long stream of faithful searchers roaming from encounter through drama to encounter with aggression tactics, from searches on mountain tops to searches through gentle water. There is a kind of one-upmanship, a prime game-playing strategy, now alive in the well-intentioned encounter movement—a concentration on the refinement of new techniques, or finding the best technique.
>
> But in a society that is wounded with the scars of endless games, it is precisely a *lack* of games that is called for. Yes, we must strip away things so as to see the essence, but we must not strip away all semblance of life in this twentieth century so as to create cloistered islands, improbable utopias, for in no way then do we have the essence of the life we lead. Therapy groups, in order to be a meaningful part of ongoing life in this society, must be representative of life in this society. And, to achieve such a purpose, one must be able to make use of the thing one has laid hold of *out*side the Deer Park and *in* the Establishment; otherwise, we have succeeded in removing some of the plague of modern existence, not out of appropriate reconstruction, but out of fairyland rockings of magic-carpet cradles in a never-never land.

Sidney Jourard, one of the more successful therapists in the encounter movement, is also one of the most lucid in expressing his own enthusiasms and doubts regarding "group." He believes that the group can provide the same type of "spiritual" experience as does the person-to-person relationship, and he has been an active participant in spreading the message of what was earlier referred to as the Esalen movement throughout the world.

In its positive manifestations the Esalen movement has been characterized by its primary goals of developing awareness and closeness in human relationships. But as the movement evolved and "growth centers" spread throughout the United States, the means toward achieving these goals came to include various techniques which involved physical touching and sexual experiences. The Allen article just quoted mentioned the "extremity" which the group movement has reached in some cases. And Jourard (1970) notes:

> I have met (or, better, *not* encountered) numerous people whom I think of as "T-group bums," or encounter group blood-hounds—who can enter a town or neighborhood, sniff the air, and say, "There's an encounter group going on somewhere," and they track it down. Once in, they cry, swear, touch, insist people stop the bullshit intellectualizing and get down to the nitty-gritty, the gut level, here-and-now, and then go home with pleasant memories, and a routine, cosmetic existence.

Despite this "artificiality," Jourard continues to support what he believes to be singular and significant in the group movement: "an experience of dialogue and encounter." He feels that the criterion of "success" in therapy has shifted from a focus on behavior to a focus on experience. Jourard (1967) clarifies his personal stance in this statement: "My commitment in the dialogue is not to a theory, technique, or setting, but to the project of abetting another person's wholeness and freedom and zestful meaning in life." Part of Jourard's own sense of responsibility to be "existential guide," with its inherent role of self-disclosure and honesty, is exemplified by his stating (1970): "The only thing I really *try* for . . . is to be available, in touch with my own state of being . . . and to disclose my state of being . . . whenever it is relevant in a dialogue between myself and whoever I am personally with just then."

We agree with Jourard's stress on responsibility. Greening alerts us to the fact that group leaders must beware of the ease with which they may "slip into a well-disguised, smoothly rationalized authoritarianism," emphasizing and pushing their own needs and biases. Lakin (1969) pointed out that the "power" of group leaders carries with it the simultaneous responsibility "to wield that power ethically and non-deceptively." He also warns against the tendency of the group leader or of various members within the group to impose "predetermined goals," such as emotional intensity or sexual awakening, on members who do not prefer this sort of endeavor. He asserts that it is highly important for group leaders to be aware of situations in which a democratic context of open and flexible decision-making is temporarily lost.

Hampden-Turner (1966) believes that when the group exercises its best potentials with continued commitment to confrontation by all participants, it permits of a mutual empathy and growth. Greening (1971) agrees, but stresses that there is no guarantee this will happen, but that the "social invention" of the encounter group is one powerful tool we have in attempting to reverse the ramifications of "man's inhumanity to man."

Rollo May was perhaps the central figure in introducing existentialism into American psychology and psychiatry. He parallels early existential philosophers in his refusal to reduce this orientation to a system; instead, he discusses existentialism as an "attitude." "An encounter," says May, "is one expression of being" that may lead to several levels of interrelationship. Perhaps the highest level is that which he terms *esteem,* "the capacity which inheres in interpersonal relations for self-transcending concern for another's welfare." Essential to May's entire approach is his stress on human dignity, ethics, and responsibility for one's actions.

Both the individual and the group encounter can therefore, when maintained within an ethical context, serve as an antidote to contemporary malaise. In the presence of a mutual caring, the syndrome of alienation, loneliness, and anxiety so rooted in our modern life is challenged. One is not "cured" from the experience of "existential loneliness," but he can learn to see it as appropriate to the reality of our times and to human existence. And, significantly, he can come to experience his personal force, and the uniting of this force with that of others, as a powerful thrust in bringing meaning out of chaos.

Other therapists within the humanistic school have been less existentially oriented in the sense of placing central emphasis on the feelings of the present moment. Some, for instance, have continued to include an initial phase of analytically oriented exploration, building toward ultimate considerations of values and goals. Charlotte Bühler feels it significant to emphasize in this later period of therapy the awareness of one's life as a whole, with goal-setting following naturally from an understanding and evaluation of one's own potentialities, as well as of specific events in the past, present, and future.

This phase parallels Ekstein's (1963) ego-developing phase of therapy in its stress on active coping and choice-making in a perspective of reality. Bühler's emphasis insists on realization of limitations as well as assets, so that the setting up of goals develops in accord with a realistic image of self, rather than an idealistic and tragic striving toward "unreachable stars" à la La Mancha (Bühler, 1968). This procedure is described vividly by Koestler in his *Ghost in the Machine* (1967). He termed this period *self-repair* in the direction and development of self-realization.

A major criticism that has been leveled against humanistic psychotherapy—as well as against psychiatry and clinical psychology—is that research on therapy to date has been unable to show predictable relationships between certain variables in therapy and resultant changes in personality as measured by such factors as no successive institutionalization (remission rate), change of scores on various personality tests, patient's self-reports, follow-up assessments by therapists, and so on. This criticism had its greatest impact as a result of the scathing commentary of H. J. Eysenck, who, in essence, questioned "the social need for the skills possessed by the psychotherapist" (1952). After comparing individuals who had been given therapy with those who had not, he concluded that there was no evidence to support the hypothesis that psychotherapy "facilitates recovery from neurotic disorder." However, Eysenck admitted to "shortcomings" in the research data relevant to this exploration and reserved final judgment until more "properly planned and executed studies" could be conducted.

In the whole of the professional literature, the only variable which seems highly correlate with a "successful" therapy is that of the client-therapist relationship. This point is mentioned by Truax and Carkhuff (1964), by Gendlin (1967), and by several other authors.

Within humanistic psychotherapy, the more "experientially" oriented psychologists see these results simply as the inability to measure or to assess a subjective situation. Representative of this phenomenological orientation is Great Britain's R. D. Laing, who, as mentioned previously, has written lucid statements on the validity and reliability of labeling and diagnosis, particularly in regard to what has become the catchall category of *schizophrenia.* Laing's books carry the message he states clearly and poetically in *The Politics of Experience* (1967): "I see you, and you see me. I experience you, and you experience me. I see your behavior. You see my behavior. But I do not and never have and never will see your experience of me . . . your experience of me is invisible to me, and my experience of you is invisible to you . . . we are both invisible men." Laing asks how natural science and psychology can try to study objectively that which is unknown to them—namely "the relation between behavior and experience." He considers it ironic that, although there is no "traditional logic" to express this relation and "no developed method of understanding its quality," we have built our science around evidence of this relation. Laing's approach is shared by many of those who would forsake *any* research with humans because of the subjective nature of man's experience and because of our inability to completely "know" one another.

Certainly our own adherence to the notion of man as an open system revolving within other systems that constantly fluctuate over time would seem to limit us in this regard. In the therapeutic situation, for instance, how does one capture all those factors which are important? And how can one evaluate the success of therapy over any group of subjects when therapy is so essentially an individual matter and each relationship is so unique? Earlier in this book we presented some attempts at achieving a methodology appropriate to this type of single-case study. We will not repeat our previous discussion. We will, however, state that, despite their lack of statistical elegance, such methods *do* exist, and people like Polanyi and other innovators are constantly at work on development of other methods, unwilling to set aside all data-collecting in regard to this important area. We ourselves feel that the therapist, if he chooses to operate within a "scientific" context, is responsible for constantly trying to assess what he does and what is happening in the therapeutic process.

The humanistic psychologist as "scientific revolutionary" is challenging the norms of traditional science. But we feel that, if he does not choose to contribute to the birth of a reformed science more appropriate to the study of the human being, he is perhaps confining himself to philosophical introspection or, in some cases, an even more narrow solipsism. One can justifiably choose any of these positions. We personally believe that man's experience is both rational and irrational and that behavior can be seen and studied both objectively and subjectively. We have chosen to continue seeking new methods for the study of the person.

The position of humanistic psychotherapy in the spectrum of modern psychotherapy is well illustrated through the results of a recent "critical review of issues, trends, and evidence" by Strupp and Bergin (1969). One statement central to this paper is: "It has become increasingly clear that psychotherapy as currently practiced is not a unitary process and is not applied to a unitary problem." In other words, and in line with the questions we have posed previously, Strupp and Bergin feel that "specific therapeutic interventions produce specific changes in specific patients under specific conditions." They summarize their findings in this direction with the following conclusions:

a. Therapists cannot be regarded as interchangeable units.
b. Patients, depending upon variables in their personality, education, intelligence, the nature of their emotional problems, motivation, and other factors, are differentially receptive to different forms of therapeutic influence.
c. Technique variables cannot be dealt with in isolation, but must be viewed in the context of patient and therapist variables enumerated above.
d. Outcome measures are frequently restricted to dimensions derived from specific theoretical positions and thus evidence based upon such measures is difficult to generalize.

In light of these insights, Strupp and Bergin state that the success of "psychotherapy in general" cannot be assessed usefully. Instead, they compare the relative merits of different procedures, specifically those of psychoanalytic therapy, client-centered therapy, and behavior therapy. However, they conclude that more research is needed, in which therapist characteristics and techniques and client variables are studied intensively.

Interestingly enough, a book by the behaviorist Mischel (1968) that has greatly influenced the field of personality assessment also concentrates on this idea of "situation specificity" but in line with reinforcement theory. We are in accord with Mischel's emphasis on "state" or process over the more traditional focus on "trait," which has about it the feeling of a static given and does not properly attend to the notion of that constantly fluctuating open system characterizing the human organism.

A critique of the work of Strupp and Bergin followed in a later issue of the *International Journal of Psychiatry*. However, two facets of their study were not challenged, and we feel they deserve attention, for they fit into the humanistic perspective. (1) Obviously, there are different approaches to helping people in the psychotherapeutic context, and many of them *can* be valid given the individual situation. The contemporary therapist does not deal only with "neurosis" and "cure" but with problems of life and living. We share with Strupp and Bergin their belief that modern psychotherapy is to a great extent an educational procedure. This is also in accord with Bugental's statement that humanistic therapy can serve as an agent for social change through reeducation. (2) Strupp and Bergin acknowledge as valid the theoretical position and procedures of humanistic psychotherapy.

In summary, humanistic psychotherapy has in its first decade developed less as a system of techniques than as an approach to human relationships in general. Regardless of the diverse opinions among members of this young school as to methodology—particularly about the degree to which *experience* is appreciated for itself rather than for its relation to life as a whole—humanistic psychologists seem to share certain emphases. They are in accord regarding the importance of the person-to-person approach; they recognize the impact of the therapist's personality and acknowledge the mutuality of the therapeutic relationship. They also share a growth-orientation. Humanistic therapists feel that the involvement of the therapist with the patient as a whole person replaces transference as a vehicle whereby the patient develops his own insights. Humanistic therapists are also in accord with their existentialist colleagues in feeling that the final decisions and choices rest with the patient. Although the therapist may support, the patient retains the basic responsibility for his life and will always be the most powerful figure in it. The therapist serves as a model in that his own life and his humanistic image of man can implicitly demonstrate to the patient his own potential for creative and positive action. At the same time, however, the humanistic ethical position suggests that he leave the patient free to express his own outlook, to develop his own goals and values. The humanistic therapist must work toward his client's freedom from dependency, toward the day he views his uniqueness as the key to a meaningful life.

B. Humanistic psychology and its applications in contemporary education

The area of education has received a great deal of attention in the last decade. The "youth revolution" of the 1960s led to a consideration of those institutions in which young people spend the greater part of their lives. Marcuse (1969) referred to the turning away of young Americans from the values of their parents as the "Great Refusal." One dictate of this New Ideology was that education, at home and in school, attend to the individual needs and integrity of the growing person.

When one attempts to sift through and integrate the literature relating to the educational process and its institutions, one is often confounded by the fact that much of it issues out of the general demand for sociopolitical revolution rather than from careful evaluations specifically directed toward innovations in education. A related source of difficulty in analyzing this literature is that much of it comes from "amateur educators," who freely profess their own expertise. Most of them have had no connection with the educational system aside from their own high school diplomas. Yet they are frequently as impassioned and certain in their analyses as were the "dime-store Freuds" of other generations. This is not to say that years spent within the American educational system may not qualify one to have some valid opinions or that any person cannot come forth with creative ideas from his life experience. If the encounter group has achieved nothing else, it has demonstrated that one does not necessarily need the credentials of a professional to sense the problems of another person and to help that person. However, many of these statements are formed impulsively, often without acknowledging the complexity of the problems. Similarly, the certainty with which many individuals blithely prescribe panaceas, refusing to search for or admit to loopholes in their solutions, is highly suspect.

It seems foolhardy to profess absolute certainty in relation to *any* area which concerns the administration of education to many individuals who come together somewhat at random to form a group and are then fitted into a larger group with a wide range of ages and needs. This situation, which is that of the American public school, places us in confrontation with a system of so many elements, a system so open and unpredictable, that the most careful plan or ardent ideology is threatened.

As in humanistic psychotherapy, the humanistic educator's deep concern is not with a formulated set of techniques but with the goal of growth. All the factors we discussed in relation to therapy and therapeutic interactions are appropriate in relation to education. The humanistically oriented individual asks, in regard to education: "What is our aim in educating our children?" "What *are* we (and) what are we to do with our lives?" asks George B. Leonard in his frank and challenging book *Education and Ecstasy* (1968). "Whenever we do anything about education," he says, "we are forced up against the ultimate definitions, the ultimate questions." And these questions are those issuing out of that universally humanistic inquiry we have asked both implicitly and explicitly throughout this book: *What is a human being? What is the humanistic image of man?*

We must also ask if our own particular philosophy of man, once arrived at, carries with it a belief that man should develop in a certain way. If so, do we then impose this belief on others through the training and conditioning process? Mechanistically oriented scientists have been criticized for their attempts at manipulation and control. But what of our own manipulations? These are weighty issues, and many of them remain unresolved.

The central purpose of our study of these problems will be to define the range of current thought regarding education that seems to manifest the humanistic ethic. Relevant contributions come from many sources—from psychologists and statesmen, from those educated formally and those self-educated, from professors and students. We will present examples we feel to be representative.

Critics of the educational system currently emphasize two main points: (1) the American life-style and (2) the lack of regard for individuality and the related need for humanistic reform in our schools.

1. A first area of concentration focuses on dissection of our life-styles and the effect on the growing youngster of culturally accepted ways of living and modes of upbringing. Even a cursory look at the "American pattern" reveals that many people experience high levels of anxiety, loneliness, alienation, and despair. Their own identities threatened, they wander lost, without root or direction, the vast society rattling around them. The nurturing of emotional health or psychological well-being (Bradburn, 1969) is the central goal of many persons involved in the question of education. Here we note a growing concern for the entire course of life as educational development, not confining the idea of learning to the classroom. This is, of course, akin to the humanistic perspective.

This line of study was engendered by the work of C. Bühler (1933) on the "Course of Human Life" and by the discussions of Goldstein, Horney, and Fromm on healthy versus sick endgoals. The subject was thoroughly investigated by Maslow in his important book *Motivation and Personality* (1954). The culmination of this initial era of consideration came with Marie Jahoda's attempt to define mental health (1958).

The impact of psychoanalysis instilled guilt and fear of failure in American parents, and in the late 1940s the public began to seek easy-to-understand and jargon-free advice on how to raise children. Books popular with a broad spectrum of Americans were those presenting "practical procedures for handling situations which commonly arise." The best known of its time was that of Dr. Benjamin Spock (1946), and this lineage has continued to the currently well-known dialogues of H. Ginott (1965).

2. A second major criticism directed against the educational system has to do with its failure to attend to each individual, to help each individual develop as a person.

All too often the patient in therapy asserts that his parents never recognized him or treated him as a person, *as himself,* and that he was never given the feeling of integrity and dignity necessary for self-worth. This accusation has now spread to educational institutions. Recognition of each individual's need for a feeling of self-worth is certainly the basis of all upbringing, of all education, of all positive growth.

Because humanistic psychologists see the educational process as continuous throughout life, those who treat education from this perspective are dealing with how the child comes to know himself and others and how both parents and teachers perceive and develop each child's unique potentials and accept his particular limitations. Although this humanistic plea for growth often seems directed at the school, it is also implicitly intended for the family, the government, and all other institutions whose powerful hands can affect the potentials of the developing individual.

Willis Harman (1971), noted Stanford educator, has written on the macroproblems of the world and, with his ecological approach, demonstrates that systems for education exist within those greater systems which must be changed for the survival of man as human. As indicated earlier, the sociopolitical revolutionary effort has served to point the finger at education. We believe that the adoption of a humanistic attitude toward reforming our educational system is, by now, the rule rather than the exception.

Harman comments that if this humanistic transformation takes place in our culture, education will be a vastly different undertaking. He states that the process would be akin to that of the "Perennial Philosophy," a classical concept which entails "discovering for oneself that part of one's self that goes on." Harman believes that the tenets of this philosophy are largely those of delineating the importance of levels of choice. An individual educated in a humanistically transformed culture would be directed toward "becoming authentically man" (Harman, 1971).

The first revolutionary "humanistic" system of education to gain wide attention was perhaps that of Great Britain's A. S. Neill (1960), who presented his concept of *Summerhill,* "a radical approach to child rearing," in both theoretical form and in his unique application, the Summerhill schools themselves. Neill wants children to be educated "without fear." His permissive approach does not, however, mean freedom without limits. In writing the foreword to Neill's book, Erich Fromm (1960) made himself an apostle of the Summerhill approach. He sketched the evolution of a child's education "without force" as emerging from the progressive thought of the eighteenth century, which favored freedom instead of authority. This method of "appealing to (the child's) curiosity and spontaneous needs, and thus (getting) him interested in the world around him" is inherent in the credo of contemporary humanistic psychologists.

Fromm summarizes what he considers to be the main factors in Neill's system:

1. Neill maintains a firm faith in "the goodness of the child."
2. The aim of education, like the aim of life, should be to work joyfully and to find happiness (which Neill defines as an interest in life).
3. Education must develop a child not only intellectually, but also emotionally.
4. The child is not yet an altruist and cannot as yet love others as an adult does.
5. Discipline and punishment are harmful because they create fear and hostility.
6. Freedom does not mean license; there must be mutual respect between child and grown-up.
7. There should be sincerity on the part of the teacher.
8. The child must learn to face the world and later to break his ties with the parents.
9. Guilt feelings are an impediment to independence and bind the child to authority.
10. Summerhill offers a value education as an alternative to religion.

Particularly in regard to this last point, Neill was prophetic in delineating the rehumanization of our culture. Neill writes in *Summerhill:*

> The battle is not between believers in theology and nonbelievers in theology; it is between believers in human freedom and believers in the suppression of human freedom . . . some day a new generation will not accept the obsolete religion and myths of today. When the new religion comes, it will refute the idea of man's being born in sin. A new religion will praise God by making man happy.

Certainly Neill demonstrates his dedication to a humanistic credo by favoring an educational system which offers freedom to develop one's potentials. But the humanistic plea is also for individual growth through constructive contributions and sensitivity to others. Thus there must also be self-discipline, self-control, and delay of personal gratification. And here, Neill, whose schools worked possibly because of his unique warmth, spontaneity, and motivation, leaves us with questions. How do his children learn those values beyond self and self-indulgence? How do they recognize the long-term value of immediate compromise? How are they able to return to the greater society and integrate what they have learned with the functioning of that society?

We might note that these are the same questions we were forced to ask regarding "far-out" extensions of the encounter group movement. Here lie the basic problems of *all* free education —problems we believe have still not been answered. How does one present the importance of goals and values? How does one accomplish the development of self-discipline within a permissive and sometimes hedonistically oriented system?

If we abandon training our children to be sensitive to, relate to, and give and take with others, we leave the universal arena of humanity and journey inward again into the narrow confines of a distorted form of self-centeredness. In essence, then, we are no longer ethical humanists.

One must stress here that the very uniqueness and individuality for which people like A. S. Neill fight speak to us intuitively, telling us that one man's Summerhill is another man's P.S. 108, that while some children cry out for less-structured and more self-determined existences, others need some manner of guidance. The Summerhill style of freedom may be for many a burden with which they cannot cope.

In this respect we are skeptical of the statements by G. B. Leonard (1968), with whom we agree in many other ways. Leonard is, like Neill, idealistic in assuming that "learning is sheer delight" for everybody, that "learning itself is life's ultimate purpose." As long as even a vestige of our contemporary culture remains, there will be masses of people who are content *not* to learn and who confront new things only with great anxiety. Joseph Katz (Katz et al., 1968) concurs with us in stating that, while "self-determination by a student ought to be a cardinal principle from the beginning," students "are greatly differentiated from each other . . . in their ability and interests . . . their purposes, learning styles, backgrounds, and personalities." As we have learned to recognize so well in the psychotherapeutic context and have tried to demonstrate in this book, what works for one person does not necessarily work for, or even relate to, another.

Therefore we cannot help being dubious about criticisms of "the system" that are overgeneralized. Many of them employ what is by now the highly developed rhetoric of the "revolution," often masking their failure to consider the specific detail of any problem. We are in sympathy with the underlying expressions of many of these writers, who in many instances have risked their personal status to expose dehumanizing features in the system. But their brand of anarchistic thought does not propose new structures to replace the dated and the decadent.

Many young professors have been disenchanted with the arena which they entered with high ideals and expectations. Finding their own spontaneity and creative ideas stifled along with those of their students, many of them spoke out against the inequities of the "oppressive" system. Using the stark simile of "the student as nigger," Jerry Farber (1969) wrote one of the best-known of these dialogues:

> School is where you let the dying society put its trip on you. Our schools may seem useful: To make children into doctors, sociologists, engineers—to discover things. But they're poisonous as well. They exploit and enslave students; they petrify society; they make democracy unlikely. And it's not *what* you're taught that does the harm, but *how* you're taught.

Farber preaches his *own* brand of permissiveness: "If schools were autonomous and were run by the people in them, then we could learn without being subdued and stupefied in the process, and perhaps, we could regain control of our own society."

But an inflamed rhetoric sometimes threatens the inherent power of Farber's statements, which to some are unappealing because of their echo of adolescent rebellion without productivity: "Students can change things if they want to, because they have the power to say 'No.' When you go to school, you're doing society a favor."

Farber and writers of his orientation are most potent when they concentrate on that specific process described by social-learning theorists as external reinforcement, as opposed to internal, or self, reinforcement.

Farber describes the educational system as

> twelve years in a Roman circus wherein the winners get gold
> stars, affection, envy; they get A's and E's, honors, awards, and
> college scholarships. The losers get humiliation and degradation.
> The fear of losing the game is a great fear. It's the fear of swats,
> of the principal's office, and above all the fear of failing.

Perhaps even more tragic than the school's emphasis on success
and competition is the fact that this "authority addiction" is incul-
cated into the parents, who "pay their kids for A's and punish
them for D's and F's."

Two young professors named Robertson and Steele jeop-
ardized their positions at Long Beach State by writing *The Halls
of Yearning* (1969), "a manifesto of student liberation" and indict-
ment of a system of education which "inoculates people against
learning by giving them injections of a weakened, artificial copy
of the real thing." They emphasize, however, that the schools are
only symbolic of "the whole thing [which is] a farce and must be
rebuilt, starting with the foundations."

Rollo May (1967) also considers this aspect as part of his
discussion of the "human dilemma." But his statement is clearly
one step removed from the more familiar rhetoric of the revolution, for he never loses sight of his own ethic of personal responsibility. He speaks of the educational institution as a primary source
of learned *anxiety* and *disappointment* in the growing human being.

> *The student's values are inevitably shifted to external signs.* He is
> validated by scores; he experiences himself of worth only in
> terms of a series of marks on a technical scale. This shift of
> validation to the outside shrinks his consciousness and under-
> mines his experience of himself. And again it is not simply that
> the criteria are external (we all must live, at whatever stage, by
> many external criteria) but rather criteria are not *chosen by the
> person himself* but brought to bear upon him by others, in this
> case parents and school authorities.

May's approach is our own. It carries within it the notion that
when one chooses his own requirements and methods of accomplishment, these criteria, whether external or internal, have more
meaning than those imposed by others.

Theodore Roszak (1969) is also in sympathy with this
position. And Paul Goodman (1962), who is certainly radical in his

sociopolitical approach, also expresses our belief that "self-government" and "autonomy" in the educational system are not necessarily sufficient for an innovative and productive learning environment. Goodman writes:

> Put it this way: There are 1900 colleges and universities; at least several hundred of these have managed to collect faculties that include many learned and creative adults who are free to teach what they please; all 1900 are centers of lively and promising youth. Yet one could not name ten that strongly stand for anything peculiar to themselves, peculiarly wise, radical, experimental, or even peculiarly dangerous, stupid, or licentious. It is astounding that there should be so many self-governing communities, yet so much conformity to the national norm. How is it possible?

Goodman asks this question again in his own journals (1966), saying: "Why are we so well behaved?" In answering, he affirms our idea that "frigidity" and "inflexibility" in the culture are so pervasive as to exclude easy answers.

Although we are definitely allied with the aforementioned writers in their emphasis on internal development, on self-reinforcement, and on the frailties of a system which perpetuates blind authority and competitiveness, we are also critical in the following regard. Most writers of a New Left orientation have, as we mentioned, been so enmeshed in the tangle of their own rhetoric, so overwhelmed by their passions, that they fail to be selective or consistent. Initially, the broad and frequently shocking nature of their accusations served to shake people out of their lethargy, to activate apathetic students, to challenge the cloistered educator. By now these accusations in their generality are as familiar in our culture as certain slogans and TV commercials. We do not mean that many of these criticisms lack validity. But without specifically oriented critics who can analyze and suggest appropriate change, all the passionate rhetoric is reduced to the embryonic whisper from which it grew.

In the late 1960s, due largely to the force of the Vietnam protest and the reality of gross inequities in American culture, many prominent figures came gradually to align themselves with certain facets of the youth movement.

In analyzing and reinforcing the right to dissent as part of our heritage, Supreme Court Justice William O. Douglas (1970) saw many of youth's "points of rebellion" as highly pertinent; he called this period a "new renaissance," stating that "a minimum necessity was measurable change." In relation to the American university, which had become the central arena for youth's struggle, he recommended that these schools be separated from government interference in the manner of "CIA and Pentagon control, through grants of money or otherwise." Speaking of education on the campus, Douglas wrote, "Faculties and students should have the basic control so that the university will be a revolutionary force that helps shape the restructuring of society. A university should not be an adjunct of business, nor of the military, nor of government. *Its curriculum should teach change, not the status quo*" (italics ours).

As mentioned earlier, much of the focus on the American educational institution resulted from the sometimes sensationalized aspect of youth confronting authority in its own backyard. This situation is analogous to the initiation of the black people's struggle with its symbolic gesture of burning down their own neighborhoods, homes, and shops, which had helped to shelter and feed them but had also caged and impoverished them.

The peak event in America's student revolution was the united effort of 400 colleges against the government's invasion of Cambodia. The Student Strike of May 1970 opened the door for youth to address the authorities of the country and the university on many questions after they had successfully refused to go back to class and risked loss of college, degrees, parental approval, and so on. We shall discuss this event later as a classic moment of truth in which masses of young people were confronted with a situation where assessment and balancing of priorities and values had to be accomplished quickly and carefully (Allen, 1970d). Two major tragedies happened within the initial week of the strike: state troops killed students at Kent State in Ohio, and state police killed students of Jackson State in Mississippi. Within the month the President had called for a Commission on Campus Unrest to analyze the sources of dissent.

In its recommendations to the government, faculty, administrators, students, police, and troops, the Scranton Commission discusses the revolt on the campus as one "which reflects and increases a more profound crisis in the nation as a whole." It delineates two basic dimensions, a crisis of violence and a crisis of understanding, the latter of which is described as more widespread and revealing.

The Scranton Commission (1970) directs its overview past that of a mass of youth in protest and past the impassioned rhetoric which we believe has often hurt the movement. The following statement summarizes that aspect of the commission's report with which we are most in accord and which is most in accord with the humanistic perspective we have attempted to present in this book:

> It is a misconception that campus unrest is a specific problem whose specific cause is moral failure and which therefore has a specific solution . . . In and of itself campus unrest is not a problem and requires "no solution." The existence of dissenting opinions and voices is simply a social condition, a fact of modern life; the right of such opinion to exist is protected by our Constitution . . . it is not a single or uniform thing. Rather it is the aggregate result, or sum, of hundreds and thousands of individual beliefs and discontents, each of them unique as the individuals who feel them. These individual feelings reflect in turn a series of choices each person makes about what he will believe, what he will say, and what he will do.

The Commission is, however, united in viewing the youth culture as a movement having at its center "the romantic celebration of human life, of the unencumbered individual, of the senses, and of nature." This culture is seen as rejecting the operational ideals of American culture, such as "materialism, competition, rationalism, technology, consumerism, and militarism." The report is a careful integration of relevant literature and experience.

Perhaps the stellar example of integration regarding the problems of education as a whole in the United States is presented by Charles Silberman (1970), who, under the aegis of a Carnegie Corporation grant, did a long-term study of teacher education, later relating this to the culture as a whole. The effect on each person of the manner in which the culture informs and educates is a process which the Greeks called the *paideia.* Silberman states that "the weakness of American education is not that the *paideia* does not educate, but that it educates to the wrong ends." Silberman's basic criticism, supported with careful and precise data and logically developed, consistent thought, is in essence that the

American school system is not purposeful and that we must be concerned with that reformation in education which would attend to the quality of minds who are capable of discovering knowledge for themselves. Furthermore, education has failed the society's basic test of any institution: "whether it is adequate to the needs of the present and of the foreseeable future." Education has failed for Silberman in that its origins are "task-oriented and job-specific" and do not therefore have that "purposefulness" which guides and models growth toward individual creativity, purpose, and meaning. Silberman does not, however, play the prophet of doom, for he sees American institutions as moving, as improving, along with the society.

The recent commentary of John Cantelon (1969), Dean of Letters and Sciences at the University of Southern California, also addresses this problem. Cantelon feels that the waning of interest in the humanities with emphasis on the sciences resulted in the failure of the university to help its students treat the two fundamental questions "What is man?" and "Who am I?" Cantelon sketches what he calls an "immodest proposal" for a "humane university" wherein self-knowledge and world-knowledge are not incongruous. He joins Silberman in asserting that "the integration of knowledge is not in the curriculum, however new and exciting, but in the student's mind." He also reinforces our position that the university and its students cannot divorce themselves from the community.

We join these educators in recognition of those active applications which are taking place in public schools and universities all over the country and which *must* be followed by later evaluation, for modified systems that are to work must build within them the facility for future change.

What are some of these changes? We mention only a few, believing them to be representative of trends and perspectives in humanistic psychology.

Carl Rogers (1970) and Charlotte Bühler (1969) have long favored the incorporation of encounter-group procedures *within* the process of education. In *Freedom to Learn* Rogers presents the results of this approach in some settings and pleads for the continuation of certain directed forms of experiential learning and education.

Barbara Mullens (1971), of the Counseling Center at the American University in Washington, D.C., has described a working program of great scope wherein several thousand students each obtain various types of counseling as a regular part of their university life. In this setting, humanistic psychologists have joined with behaviorists and Freudians to pool knowledge toward making "the traditional counseling center into a center of consciousness."

We are impressed by the fact that several behavioristically oriented psychologists have utilized their expertise in the area of learning and reinforcement to enter directly into classrooms and tailor-make appropriate programs for the treatment of both individual and group problems. Among those prominent in this respect are Frank Hewett and Frederick Kanfer. We join George Leonard in feeling that the creative utilization of technology toward the freeing of the individual is only secondarily manipulative. It can well be defined as "humanizing" and humanistic. Camp loyalties are transparent in an era when team effort and pooling of knowledge are required so that we may use whatever tools we have to best achieve our ends.

On many campuses throughout the country, tradition is bending toward the inclusion of faculty and students as voting members of college boards of trustees. Highly progressive schools such as Sonoma State in California work toward more extreme forms of self-governance. Students are freed to formulate their own graduate education, educating themselves totally in the field and out of the classroom if they wish.

The Santa Cruz system, which is free from grades and operates on a pass-fail basis, has demonstrated that students can do their undergraduate work in this system and still be prepared for and accepted at major graduate schools in our country.

Carl Rogers (1963) pointed out several years ago the emasculation of psychology students in the process of graduate training. They are frequently treated as "manipulative objects" whose passing of exams is the criterion for their "selection and for judging professional promise." We have mentioned the now common criticism that our universities have abdicated their connection with the community. Albert Marston, Director of Clinical Training at the University of Southern California, conceived a program in which clinical psychology students are trained as community problem solvers and consultants. Both faculty and graduate students joined in the formulation of this new model.

In all these ways, individuals have begun to resist that static structure which turns dull and passive "the best minds of our generation" (Ginsberg, 1957). All these attempts recognize the importance of helping the individual formulate his own values toward living a meaningful life.

The humanistically oriented educational system is geared toward the production of "radical" men of the Maslow/Hampden-Turner description—in that young individuals would be fearless of change, risking both conformity and nonconformity. Rather than withdraw from contact with the frightening and chaotic contemporary world, they would brandish themselves as weapons in resistance to dehumanizing aspects of this world.

In two papers directed toward analysis of the "rebel," with focus on the Student Strike of 1970 as "moment of truth," Allen (1970d, 1971) presented stages in the development of American youth in revolution. The "Freudian rebel" was sketched as the hedonistically oriented "tripper." The "American rebel" typically invests in a cause that chances to "win" or to "pay off." He packages a cause as his product. The highest level of revolt was delineated as that in which the rebel is humanistically oriented, acting out of conscience and commitment to universal ideals. Allen distinguished between "consciousness," a popular keyword in the rhetoric of the revolution, and "conscience."

> *Consciousness* and *conscience* are representative of distinctly different mechanisms in the human being . . . Whereas even the highest level of attainment of consciousness (or awareness) need not imply principle or commitment to what one is perceiving or experiencing . . . and may remain *internal, conscience* connotes *volitional,* deliberated operations, which direct one to *action* out of *commitment.*

Allen sees the development of a *group consciousness* among many members of the youth movement. This factor is similar to that which Riesman (Riesman, Glazer, & Denney, 1950) termed *other-directedness.* Frequently it promotes conforming behavior and is therefore antagonistic to *individual conscience* (Allen, 1971).

A recent study by Allen and Kaplan (1971) demonstrated

that a scant year after the dramatic strike of 1970, most former participants at the University of Southern California would not choose to be involved in a similar effort. Whereas self-reports the previous year had shown participants most moved by feelings of accomplishment, by the fact that they had taken a stand, thereby deriving meaning from their action, participants emphasized in retrospect the "Woodstockian" aspects of the strike as a group happening. Objection to American military presence in Southeast Asia had not changed, but "political protest," said one student, "is not where it's at."

Allen and Kaplan were not so much concerned with the lack of allegiance to political activism per se but were much affected by the rapid shift in decision to act externally out of internal principle. The USC student rated as most important to his life a personal philosophy or value system. The results of this study were therefore ironic and saddening.

Deep beliefs and personal philosophies are not, it seems, easily put aside, regardless of factors of failure and fatigue. Principle and conscience never really cool within the humanistic rebel who revolts—because he *must,* for all that is human.

Our civilization and our culture remain suspended in crisis. This sociocultural situation perpetuates a grave threat to the human race. No man can afford to abdicate his responsibility at such a time; yet many have.

The thrust of humanistic psychology to prominence as a major force in the social sciences gained impact from the humanistic psychologist's recognition that his most potent tool in the treatment of individuals, of groups, and of inadequate systems is his own humanity.

> He too is vulnerable.
> He too is exposed.
> He too is threatened.
> He is bombarded by visions both beautiful and chaotic.
> He is deafened by sounds both melodic and discordant.
> He has trembled with anxiety.
> He has been alienated to the point of turning off.
> He has withdrawn from life, hiding himself away.
> He has emerged again.
> He has thrown back his head to laugh at himself.
> He has been shot through with joy.

Bradburn, N. M. *The structure of psychological well-being.* Chicago: Aldine, 1969.

Bradford, L. P., Gibb, J. R., & Benne, K. D. (Eds.) *T-group theory and laboratory method.* New York: Wiley, 1964.

Bronowski, J. *Science and human values.* (Rev. ed.) New York: Harper & Row, 1965.

Buber, M. *I and thou.* New York: Scribner's, 1958.

Buckley, W. *Sociology and modern systems theory.* Englewood Cliffs, N. J.: Prentice-Hall, 1967.

Bugental, J. F. T. *The search for authenticity: An existential-analytical approach to psychotherapy.* New York: Holt, Rinehart, & Winston, 1965.

Bugental, J. F. T. The humanistic ethic—The individual in psychotherapy as a societal change agent. *Journal of Humanistic Psychology,* 1971, **11** (1), 11–25.

Bühler, C. *Die ersten sozialen Verhaltungsweisen des Kindes* (First Social Behavior of Infants). Jena: Quellen und Studien zur Jugendkunde 5, 1927.

Bühler, C. *Kindheit und Jugend* (Childhood and Adolescence). Leipzig: S. Hirzel, 1928.

Bühler, C. *The first year of life.* New York: J. Day, 1930.

Bühler, C. *Der menschliche Lebenslauf als psychologisches Problem* (The Course of Human Life as a Psychological Problem). Leipzig: S. Hirzel, 1933. (2nd ed.—Göttingen: Verlag für Psychologie, 1959.)

Bühler, C. Authoritarianism in Germany and Puritan U. S. A. Unpublished paper, 1941.

Bühler, C. The reality principle. *American Journal of Psychotherapy,* 1954, **8**(4), 626–647.

Bühler, C. *Values in psychotherapy.* New York: Free Press, 1962.

Bühler, C. Some observations on the psychology of the Third Force. *Journal of Humanistic Psychology,* 1965, **5**, 54.

Bühler, C. Psychotherapy and the image of man. *Psychotherapy,* 1968, **5** (2).

Bühler, C. Humanistic psychology as an educational program. *American Psychologist,* 1969, **24**(8), 736–742.

Bühler, C. Basic theoretical concepts of humanistic psychology. *American Psychologist,* 1971, **26**, 378–386.

Bühler, K. *Die Gestaltwahrnehmungen* (Gestalt Perception). Bonn: Spemann, 1913.

Bühler, K. *Die geistige Entwicklung des Kindes* (The Mental Development of the Child). Jena: G. Fischer, 1918. (5th ed.: 1929)

Bühler, K.: *Die Krise der Psychologie* (The Crisis of Psychology). Jena: G. Fischer, 1927. (American ed.—Cambridge, Mass.: Schenkman, 1967.)

Bühler, K. *Sprachtheorie. Die Darstellungsfunktion der Sprache* (Speech Theory). (2nd ed.) Stuttgart: G. Fischer, 1965.

Burton, A. *Modern humanistic psychotherapy.* San Francisco: Jossey-Bass, 1967.

Callwood, J. One sure way to happiness. *Readers' Digest,* November 1964, pp. 93–96.

Camus, A. *L'Etranger.* Paris: Librairie Gallimard, 1942.

Camus, A. *La Peste.* Paris: Librairie Gallimard, 1947.

Camus, A. *The myth of Sisyphus & other essays.* New York: Knopf, 1955.

Cantelon, J. E. *College education and the campus revolution.* Philadelphia: Westminster Press, 1969.

Cassirer, E., Kristeller, P. O., & Randall, J. H., Jr. *The Renaissance philosophy of man.* Chicago: University of Chicago Press, 1948.

Chassan, J. B. Statistical inference and the single case in clinical design. *Psychiatry,* 1960, **23,** 173–184.

Dilthey, W. *Einleitung in die Geisteswissenschaften* (Pattern and Meaning in History). 1922. American ed.—New York: Harper Torchbooks, 1961.

Douglas, W. O. *Points of rebellion.* New York: Random House, 1970.

Dukes, W. F. *N = 1. Psychological Bulletin,* 1965, **64,** 74–79.

Durkheim, E. *Le Suicide,* 1897. Current Edition: New York, Free Press, 1951. Translated by Spaulding, J. A. & Simpson, G.

Ebbinghaus, H. *Über das Gedächtnis.* Leipzig: Duncker & Bumbolt, 1885.

Eiduson, B. *Scientists: Their psychological world.* New York: Basic Books, 1962.

Ekstein, R. Pleasure and reality, play and work, thought and action. *Journal of Humanistic Psychology,* Fall 1963.

Erikson, E. Growth and crises of the "healthy personality." In M. J. E. Senn (Ed.), *Symposium on the Healthy Personality, Supplement II: Problems of Infancy and Childhood, Transactions of Fourth Conference, March 1950.* New York: Josiah Macy, Jr., Foundation, 1950.

Erikson, E. H. *Identity and the life cycle.* New York: International Universities Press, 1959.

Erikson, E. *Identity: Youth and crisis.* New York: Norton, 1968.

Eysenck, H. J. The effects of psychotherapy: An evaluation. *Journal of Consulting Psychology,* 1952, **16**(5), 319–324.

Farber, J. *The student as nigger.* North Hollywood, Calif.: Contact Books, 1969.

Fenz, W. D., & Epstein, S. Stress: In the air. *Psychology Today,* 1969, **3**(4), 28.

Feuer, L. *The conflict of generations.* New York: Basic Books, 1969.

Fitzgerald, F. *The crack-up.* New York: Scribners, 1931. (6th ed.—New York: New Directions, 1956.)

Fitzgerald, Z. Show Mr. & Mrs. F. to number. . . . *Esquire Magazine,* May & June, 1934.

Frankl, V. E. *From death-camp to existentialism. A psychiatrist's path to a new therapy.* Boston: Beacon Press, 1959.

Frankl, V. E. *Man's search for meaning.* New York: Washington Square Press, 1963.

Frankl, V. E. *The will to meaning: Foundations and applications of logotherapy.* New York: World, 1969.

Fromm, E. *Escape from freedom.* New York: Holt, Rinehart, & Winston, 1941.

Fromm, E. Foreword. In A. S. Neill, *Summerhill: A radical approach to child rearing.* New York: Hart, 1960.

Gendlin, E. Therapeutic procedures in dealing with schizophrenics. In C. Rogers (Ed.), *The therapeutic relationship and its impact.* Madison: University of Wisconsin Press, 1967.

Ginott, H. G. *Between parent and child: New solutions to old problems.* New York: Macmillan, 1965.

Ginsberg, A. Howl (a poem). *Evergreen Review,* 1957, 1(2).

Giorgi, A. *Psychology as a human science.* New York: Harper & Row, 1970.

Goldstein, K. *The organism.* New York: American Book, 1939.

Goldstein, M. J., & Adams, J. N. Coping style and behavioral response to stress. *Journal of Experimental Research in Personality,* 1967, 2(4), 239–251.

Goldstein, M. J., & Adams, J. N. Further study of coping style and behavioral response to stress. Paper presented at the Western Psychological Association Conference, Vancouver, B. C., 1969.

Goodman, P. *Compulsory miseducation and the community of scholars.* New York: Vintage, 1962.

Goodman, P. *Five years: Thoughts during a useless time.* New York: Random House, 1966.

Greening, T. C. Encounter groups from the perspective of existential humanism. In T. C. Greening (Ed.), *Existential humanistic psychology.* Monterey, Calif.: Brooks/Cole, 1971.

Hampden-Turner, C. An existential "learning-theory" and the integration of T-group research. *Journal of Applied Behavioral Science,* 1966, 2, 367–386.

Hampden-Turner, C. *Radical man.* Cambridge, Mass.: Schenkman, 1970.

Harman, W. The future of the existential-humanistic perspective in education. In T. Greening (Ed.), *Existential humanistic psychology.* Monterey, Calif.: Brooks/Cole, 1971.

Heidegger, M. *Platons Lehre von der Wahrheit, mit einem Brief über den 'Humanismus,'* Bern: A. Francke AG., 1947.

Heidegger, M. *Was ist Metaphysik?* (1929). Fifth Ed., Frankfurt: V. Klostermann, 1949.

Horner, A., & Bühler, C. Existential and humanistic psychology: A hope for the future in philosophy, psychotherapy, and research. *International Psychiatry Clinics,* 1969, 6(3), 55–73.

Horney, K. *Neurosis and human growth: The struggle toward self-realization.* New York: Norton, 1950.

Hull, C. L. *Principles of behavior.* New York: Appleton-Century-Crofts, 1943.

Jahoda, M. *Current concepts of positive mental health.* New York: Basic Books, 1958.

Jaspers, K. *Existenzphilosophie.* Berlin: Gruyter & Co., 1938.

Jourard, S. M. *The transparent self.* Princeton, N. J.: Van Nostrand, 1964.

Jourard, S. M. The psychotherapist as existential guide. Paper presented at Convention for American Humanistic Psychology, Washington, D. C., September 1, 1967.

Jourard, S. M. Education for a new society. *Forum, International Center for Integrative Studies,* 1968, **1**(4).

Jourard, S. M. The therapist as guru. *Voices,* 1969, **5**(2), 49–51.

Jourard, S. M. A way to encounter. Unpublished paper, University of Florida, 1970.

Katz, J., et al. *No time for youth: Growth and constraint in college students.* San Francisco: Jossey-Bass, 1968.

Kaufmann, W. (Ed.) *Existentialism from Dostoevsky to Sartre.* New York: Meridian, 1956.

Koch, S. (Ed.) *Psychology—A study of a science,* Vol. 3. New York: McGraw-Hill, 1959.

Koestler, A. *The ghost in the machine.* New York: Macmillan, 1967.

Kohlberg, L. Stage and sequence: The cognitive-developmental approach to socialization. In A. Croslin (Ed.), *Handbook of socialization theory and research.* New York: Rand-McNally, 1969.

Kuhn, T. S. *The structure of scientific revolution.* Chicago: University of Chicago Press, 1962.

Laing, R. D. *The politics of experience.* New York: Ballantine, 1967.

Lakin, M. Some ethical issues in sensitivity training. *American Psychologist,* 1969, **24**(10), 923–928.

Leonard, G. B. *Education and ecstasy.* New York: Dell, 1968.

Lewin, K. *Principles of topological psychology.* New York: McGraw-Hill, 1936.

Lindeman, E. *The community: An introduction to the study of community leadership and organization.* New York: Association Press, 1921.

Lorber, R., & Fladell, E. *The gap.* New York: McGraw-Hill, 1968.

Lowrie, W. *Kierkegaard.* New York: Oxford University Press, 1938.

Madsen, K. B. Humanistic psychology and the philosophy of science. Paper delivered at the First International Conference on Humanistic Psychology, Amsterdam, August 1970.

Marcuse, H. *An essay on liberation.* Boston: Beacon Press, 1969.

Maslow, A. H. *Motivation and personality.* New York: Harper & Row, 1954. (2nd ed.: 1970)

Maslow, A. H. Defense and growth. *Merrill-Palmer Quarterly,* 1956, **3**, 36–47.

Maslow, A. H. *Toward a psychology of being.* Princeton, N. J.: Van Nostrand, 1961.

Maslow, A. H. *The psychology of science. A reconnaissance.* Chicago: Henry Regnery, 1966.

Matson, F. W. *The broken image. Man, science and society.* New York: Braziller, 1964.

May, R. *Man's search for himself.* New York: Norton, 1953.

May, R. The origins and significance of the existential movement in psychology. In R. May, E. Angel, & H. Ellenberger (Eds.), *Existence.* New York: Basic Books, 1958.

May, R. *Psychology and the human dilemma.* Princeton, N. J.: Van Nostrand, 1967.

May, R. *Love and will.* New York: Norton, 1969.

May, R., Angel, E., & Ellenberger, H. F. (Eds.) *Existence: A new dimension in psychiatry and psychology.* New York: Basic Books, 1958.

McNemar, Q. Sampling in psychological research. *Psychological Bulletin,* 1940, **37,** 331–365.

Merleau-Ponty, M. *Sense and non-sense.* Evanston, Ill.: Northwestern University Press, 1964.

Milgram, S. Some conditions of obedience and disobedience to authority. *Human Relations,* 1961, **18,** 76.

Mischel, W. *Personality & assessment.* New York: Wiley, 1968.

Moustakas, C. *Loneliness.* Englewood Cliffs, N. J.: Prentice-Hall, 1961.

Mullens, B. N. The humanizing of an American University counseling center. Paper presented at the Second International Conference on Humanistic Psychology, Würzburg, 1971.

Neill, A. S. *Summerhill: A radical approach to child rearing.* New York: Hart, 1960.

Pereira, J. E. A history of volunteers in social welfare in the United States. Unpublished master's thesis, Catholic University School of Social Work, 1947.

Polanyi, M. *Personal knowledge: Towards a post-critical philosophy.* Chicago: University of Chicago Press, 1958.

Radnitzky, G. *Contemporary schools of metascience.* Göteborg: Scandinavian University Press, 1968.

Riesman, D., Glazer, N., & Denney, R. *The lonely crowd.* Hartford, Conn.: Yale University Press, 1950.

Robertson, D., & Steele, M. *The halls of yearning.* Long Beach, Calif.: Authors, 1969.

Rogers, C. *Counseling and psychotherapy.* Boston: Houghton Mifflin, 1942.

Rogers, C. *Client-centered therapy: Its current practice, implications and theory.* Boston: Houghton Mifflin, 1951.

Rogers, C. *Graduate education in psychology: A passionate statement.* Paper presented at the Western Behavioral Science Institute, 1963.

Rogers, C. *On becoming a person.* Boston: Houghton Mifflin, 1961.

Rogers, C. The process of the basic encounter group. In J. F. T. Bugental (Ed.), *Challenges of humanistic psychology.* New York: McGraw-Hill, 1967.

Rogers, C. *Freedom to learn.* Columbus, Ohio: Merrill, 1970.

Rokeach, M. *The open and the closed mind.* New York: Basic Books, 1960.

Roszak, T. *The making of a counter culture. Reflections on the technocratic society and its youthful opposition.* Garden City, N. Y.: Doubleday, 1969.

Russell, B. *A history of Western philosophy.* New York: Simon and Schuster, 1945.

Sartre, J. P. *L'Être et le Néant: Essai d'Ontologie Phénomenologique.* Paris: Librairie Gallimard, 1943.

Sartre, J. P. *L'Existentialisme est un humanisme.* Paris: Editions Nagel, 1946.

Schindler-Rainman, E., & Lippitt, R. *The volunteer community.* Washington, D. C.: Center for Voluntary Society (NTL Institute for Applied Behavioral Science), 1971.

Scott, E. M. Happiness: A comparison between delinquent and non-delinquent girls. *Psychotherapy,* 1967, **4**(2).

Scranton, W. (Chmn.) The report of the president's commission on campus unrest. Washington, D.C., 1970.

Shontz, F. C. *Research methods in personality.* New York: Appleton-Century-Crofts, 1965.

Silberman, C. E. *Crisis in the classroom.* New York: Random House, 1970.

Solzhenitsyn, A. *The cancer ward.* New York: Bantam, 1969.

Spock, B. *The common-sense book of baby and child care.* New York: Duell, Sloan and Pearce, 1946.

Strupp, H. H., & Bergin, A. E. Some empirical and conceptual bases for coordinated research in psychotherapy: A critical review of issues, trends, and evidence. *International Journal of Psychiatry,* 1969, **7**(2).

Szent-Györgyi, A. *The crazy ape.* New York: Philosophical Library, 1970.

Thomae, H. *Das Individuum und seine Welt* (The Individual and His World). Göttingen: Verlag für Psychologie, 1968.

Tolman, E. C. *Purposive behavior in animals and men.* New York: Appleton-Century-Crofts, 1932.

Truax, C. B., & Carkhuff, R. R. Significant developments in psychotherapy research. In *Progress in clinical psychology,* Vol. II. New York: Grune & Stratton, 1964.

von Bertalanffy, L. Problems of general systems theory. *Human Biology,* 1951, **23**, 302–312.

von Bertalanffy, L. General systems theory and psychiatry. In S. Arieti (Ed.), *American handbook of psychiatry,* Vol. III. New York: Basic Books, 1966.

von Bertalanffy, L. *Organismic psychology and systems theory.* Worcester, Mass.: Clark University Press (with Barre Publishers), 1968.

Wheelis, A. *The quest for identity.* New York: Norton, 1958.

Winter, E. (Ed.) *Erasmus-Luther discourse on free will.* New York: Ungar, 1961.

Yates, A. J. *Behavior therapy.* New York: Wiley, 1970.

Zubek, J. P. (Ed.) *Sensory deprivation: Fifteen years of research.* New York: Appleton-Century-Crofts, 1969.

Author index

Subject index